The
Adventures of
Strawberryhead
& Gingerbread

The Barking Lot Series ⑤

Musical Cursive Writing Workbook!

The Adventures of Strawberryhead & Gingerbread

The Barking Lot Series ⑤
Musical Cursive Writing Workbook!

KF Wheatie & KM Wheatie

Strawberryhead &
Gingerbread Press

www.strawberryheadandgingerbread.com

The Adventures of Strawberryhead & Gingerbread,
The Barking Lot Series (5) Musical Cursive Writing Workbook!

Published by Strawberryhead and Gingerbread Press
https://www.strawberryheadandgingerbread.com

ISBN: 979-8-9900656-0-4

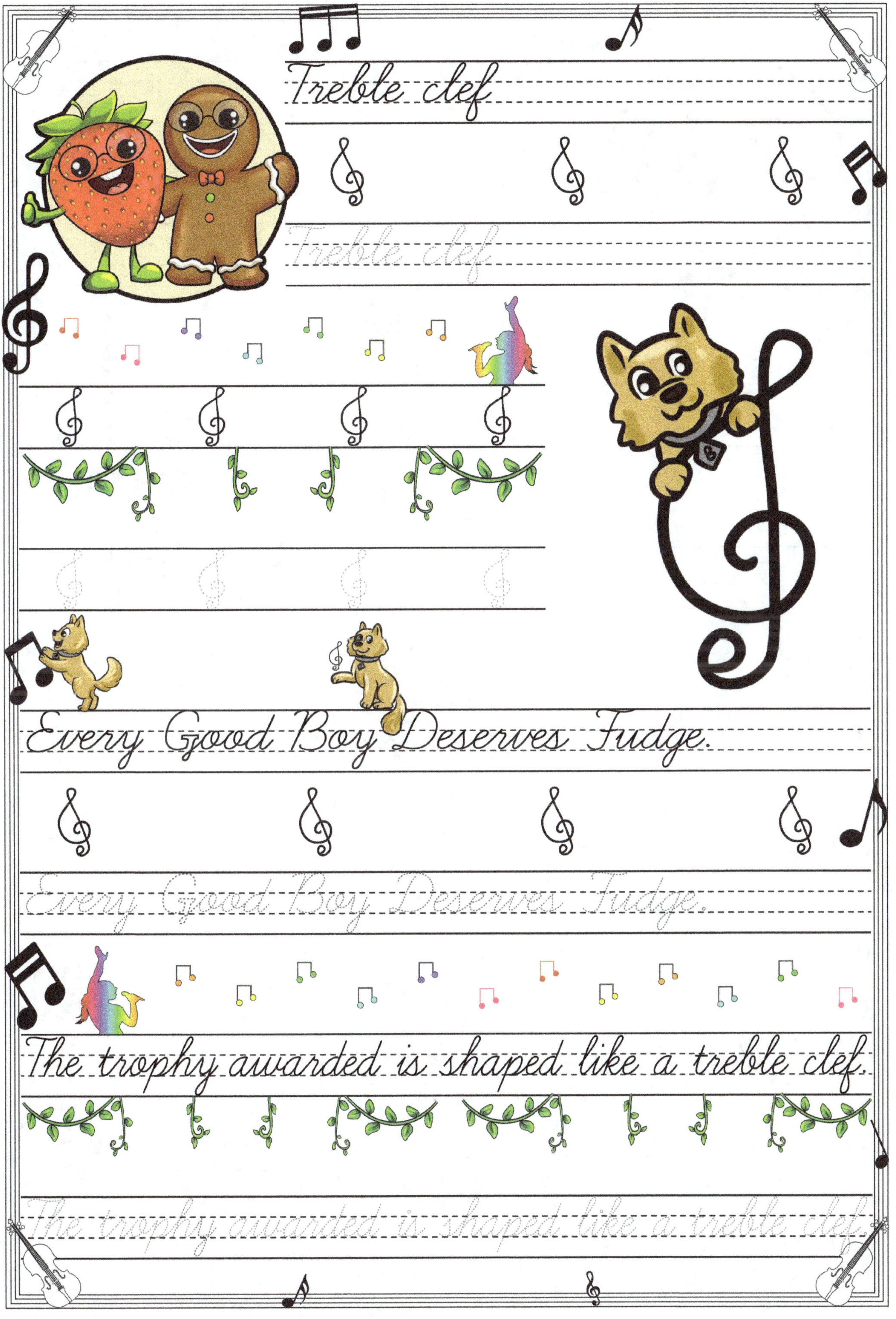

Treble clef
Treble clef
Every Good Boy Deserves Fudge.
Every Good Boy Deserves Fudge.
The trophy awarded is shaped like a treble clef.
The trophy awarded is shaped like a treble clef.

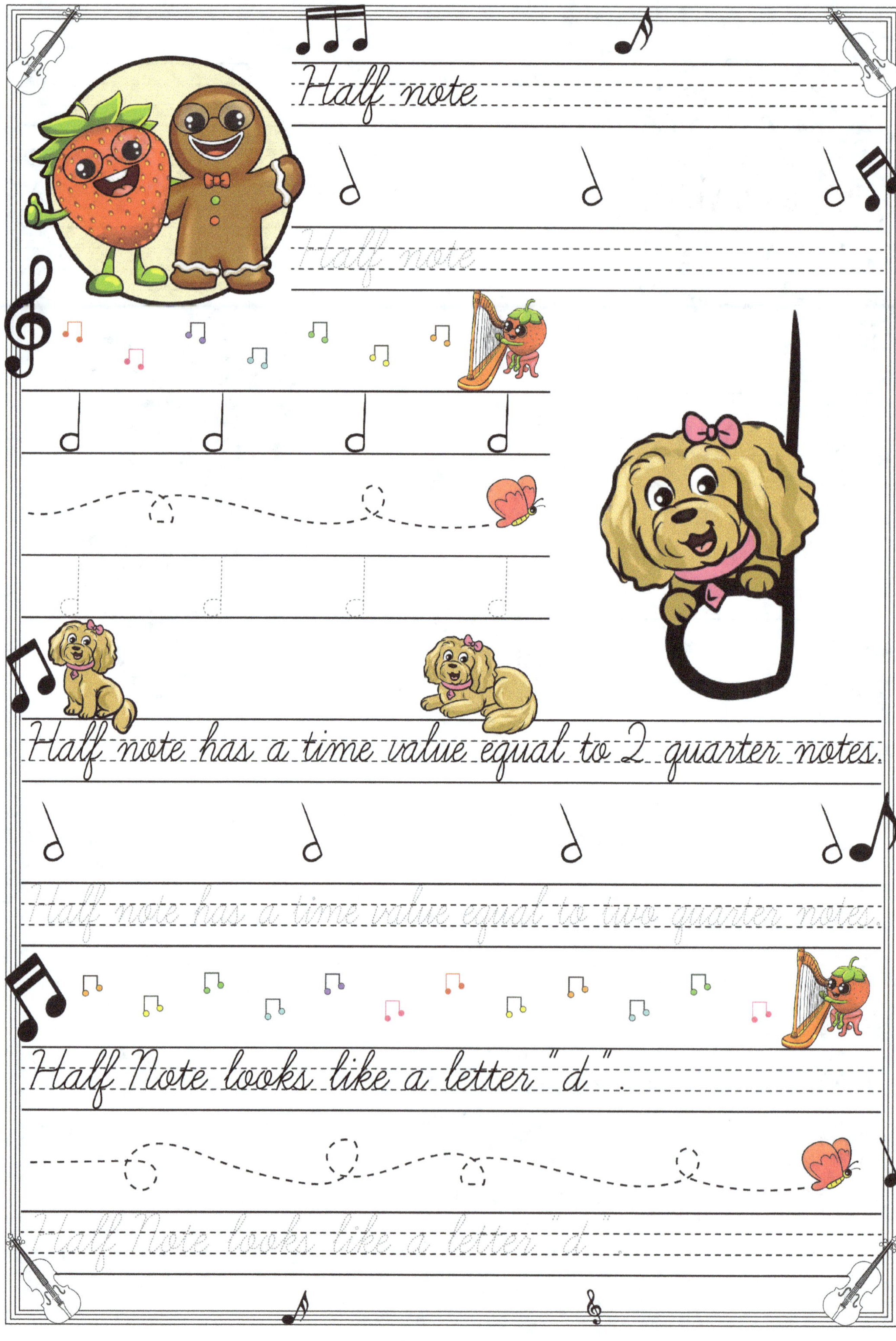

Half note

Half note

Half note has a time value equal to 2 quarter notes.

Half note has a time value equal to two quarter notes.

Half Note looks like a letter "d"

Half Note looks like a letter "d"

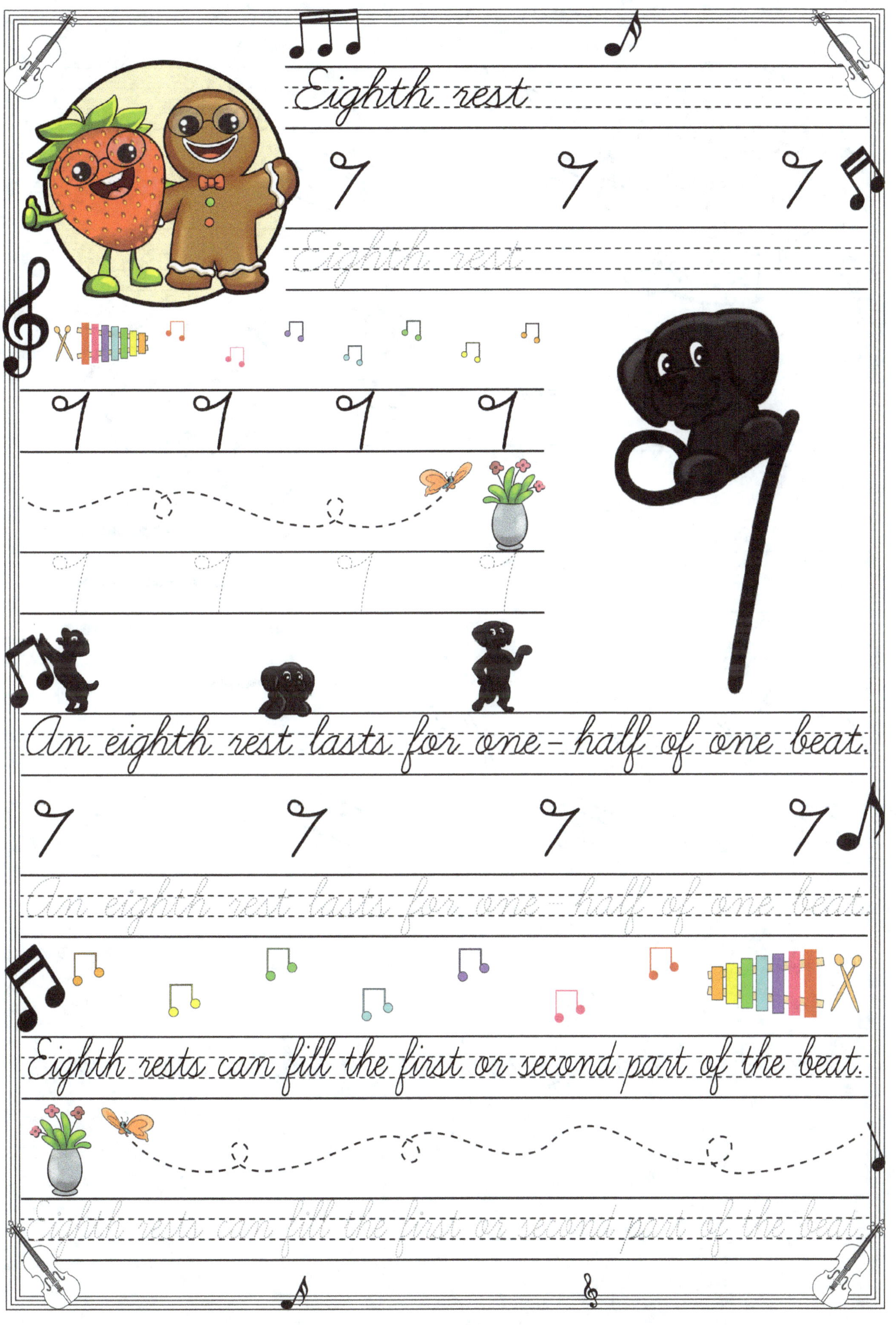
Eighth rest
Eighth rest
An eighth rest lasts for one-half of one beat.
An eighth rest lasts for one-half of one beat.
Eighth rests can fill the first or second part of the beat.
Eighth rests can fill the first or second part of the beat.

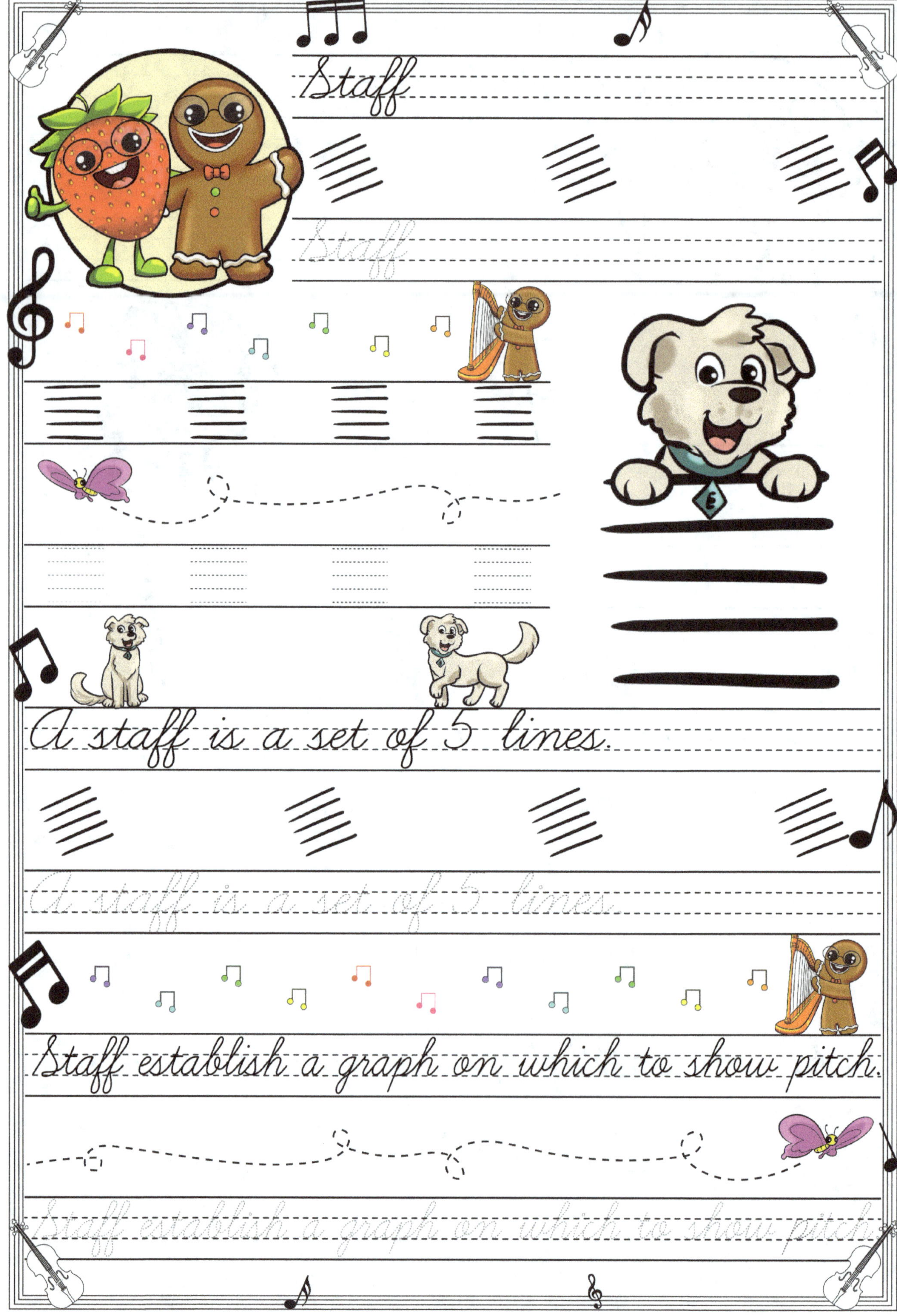

Staff

Staff

A staff is a set of 5 lines.

A staff is a set of 5 lines.

Staff establish a graph on which to show pitch.

Staff establish a graph on which to show pitch.

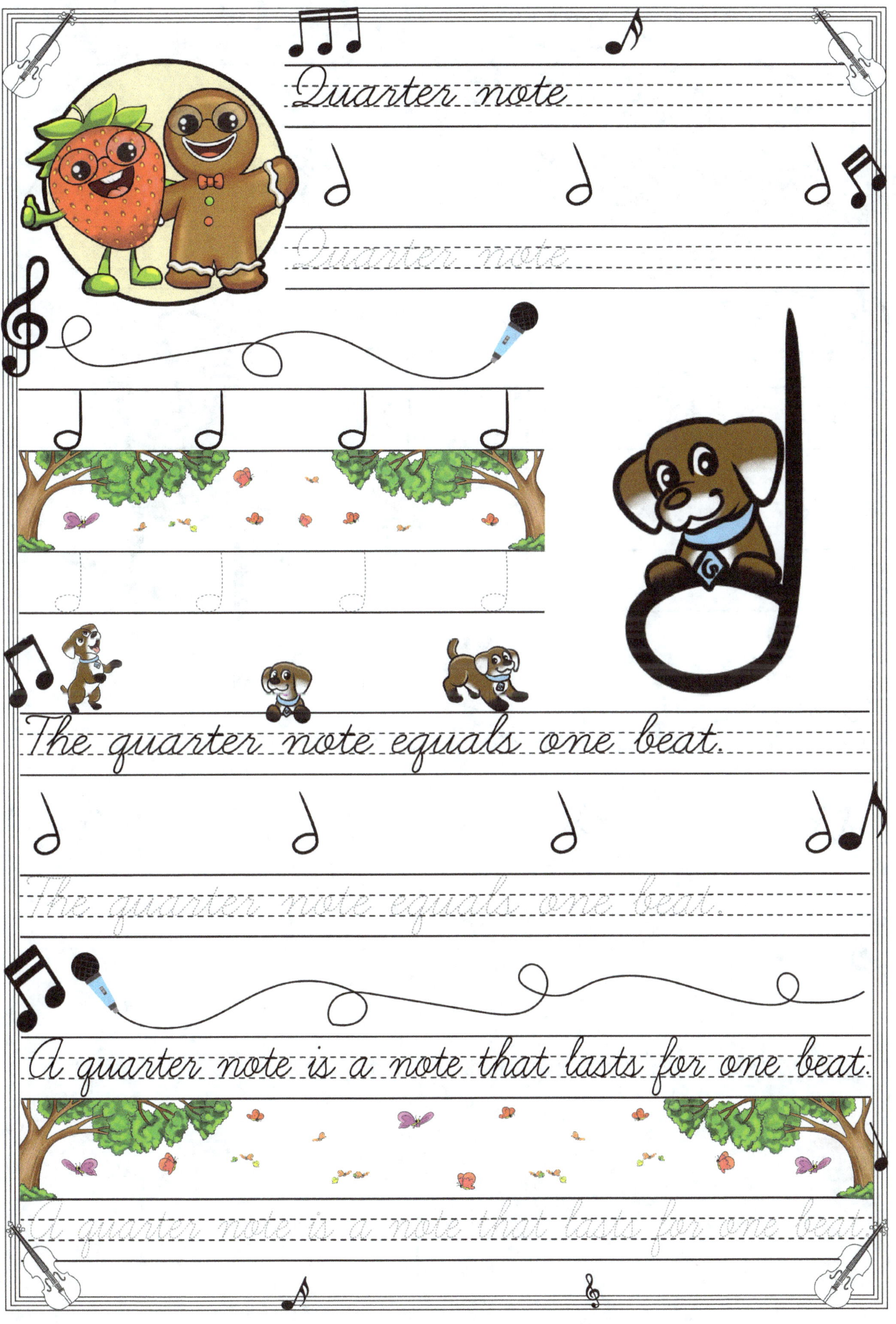

Quarter note
Quarter note
The quarter note equals one beat.
The quarter note equals one beat.
A quarter note is a note that lasts for one beat.
A quarter note is a note that lasts for one beat.

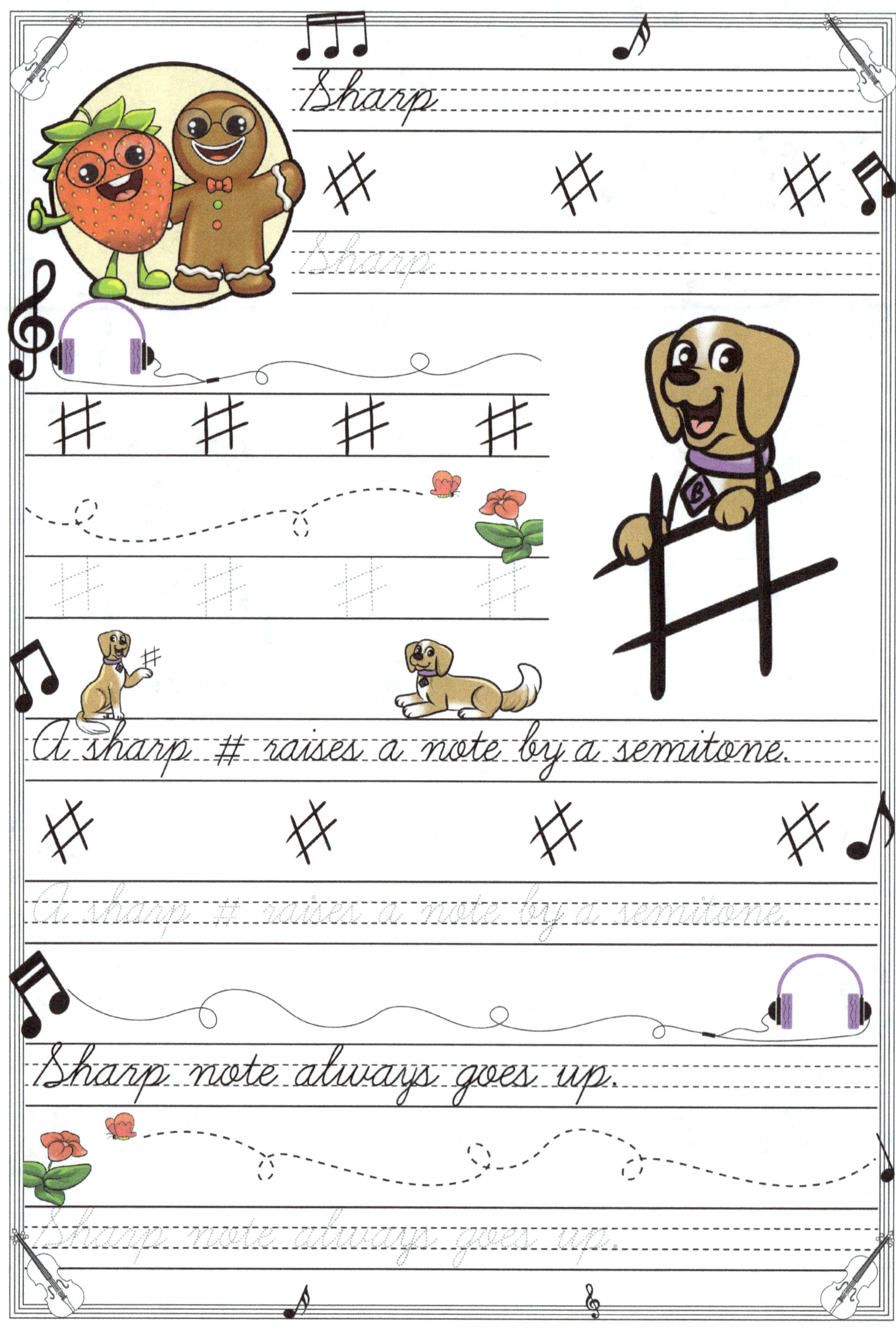

Sharp
Sharp
A sharp # raises a note by a semitone.
A sharp # raises a note by a semitone.
Sharp note always goes up.
Sharp note always goes up.

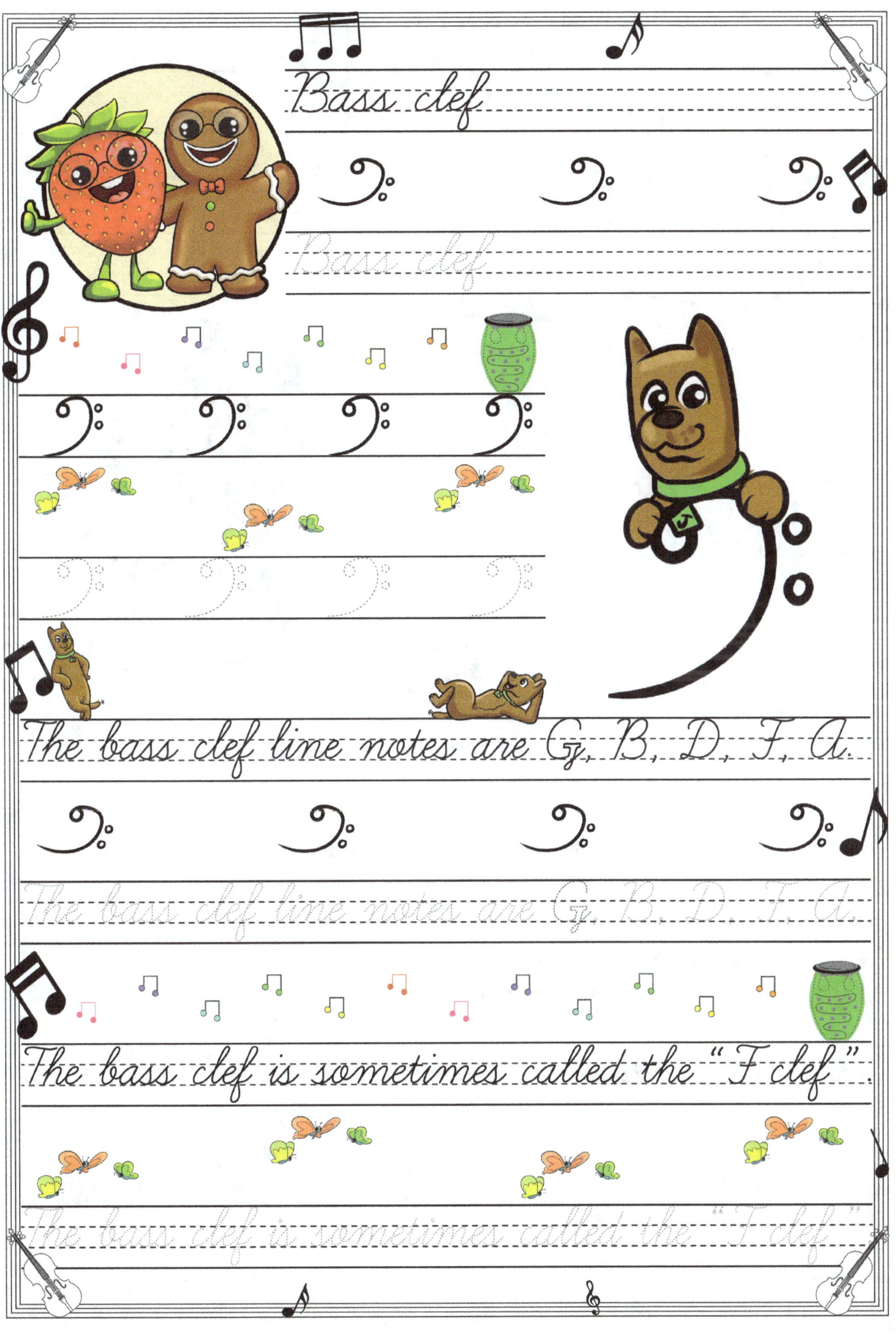

Bass clef
Bass clef
The bass clef line notes are G, B, D, F, A.
The bass clef line notes are G, B, D, F, A.
The bass clef is sometimes called the "F clef".
The bass clef is sometimes called the "F clef".

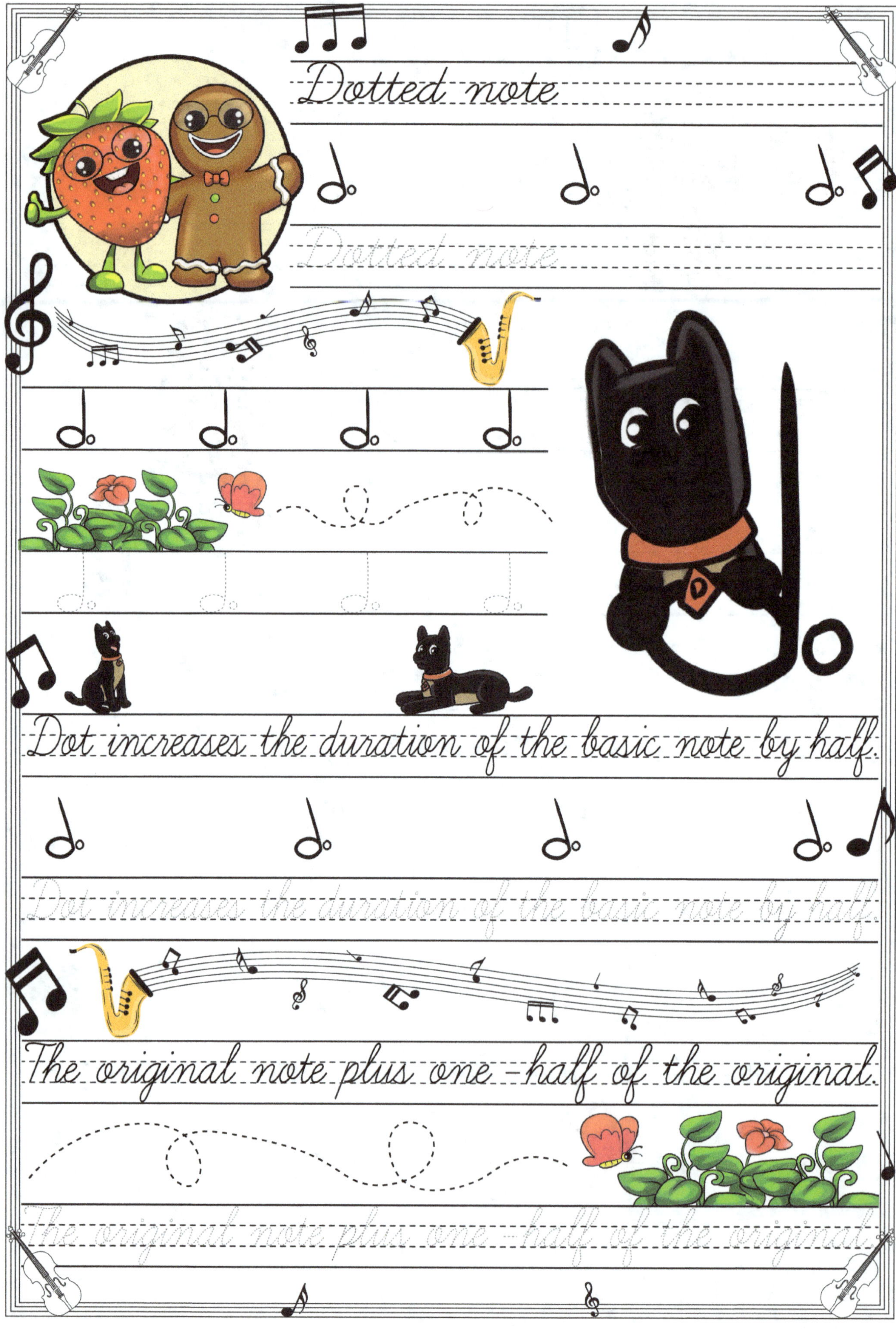

Dotted note

Dotted note

Dot increases the duration of the basic note by half.

Dot increases the duration of the basic note by half.

The original note plus one-half of the original.

The original note plus one-half of the original.

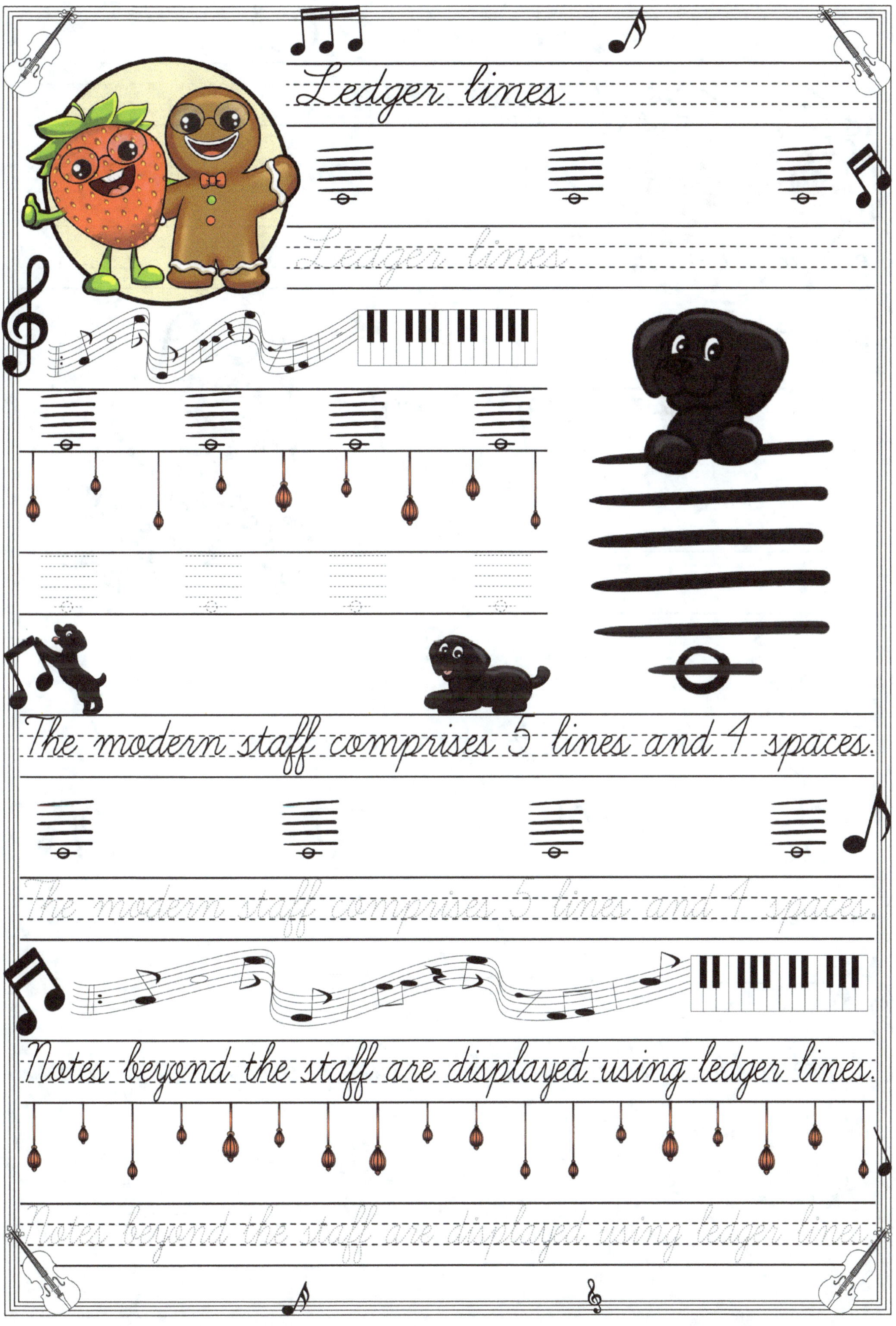

Ledger lines
Ledger lines
The modern staff comprises 5 lines and 4 spaces.
The modern staff comprises 5 lines and 4 spaces.
Notes beyond the staff are displayed using ledger lines.
Notes beyond the staff are displayed using ledger lines.

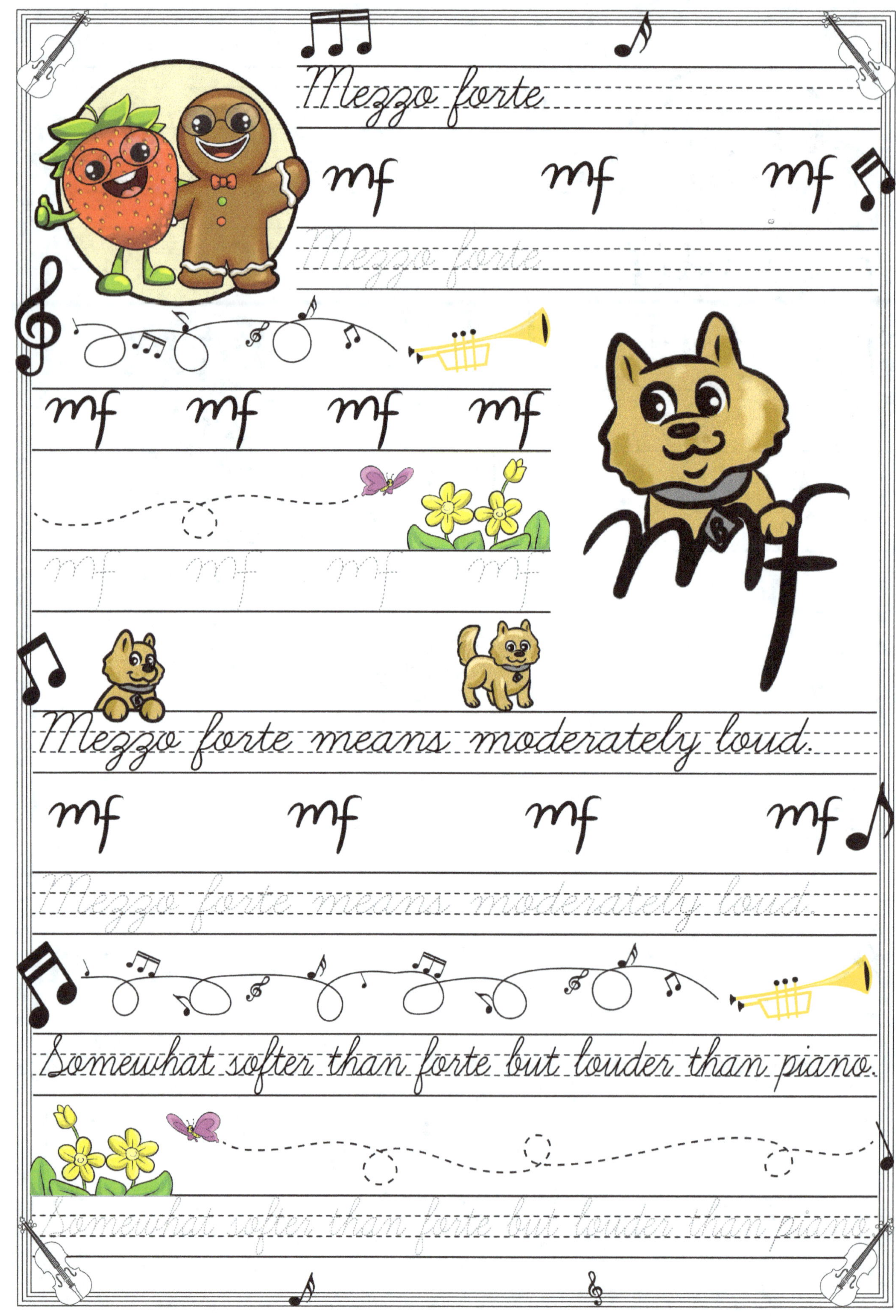
Mezzo forte
mf   mf   mf
Mezzo forte
mf   mf   mf   mf
mf   mf   mf   mf
mf
Mezzo forte means moderately loud.
mf   mf   mf   mf
Mezzo forte means moderately loud.
Somewhat softer than forte but louder than piano.
Somewhat softer than forte but louder than piano.

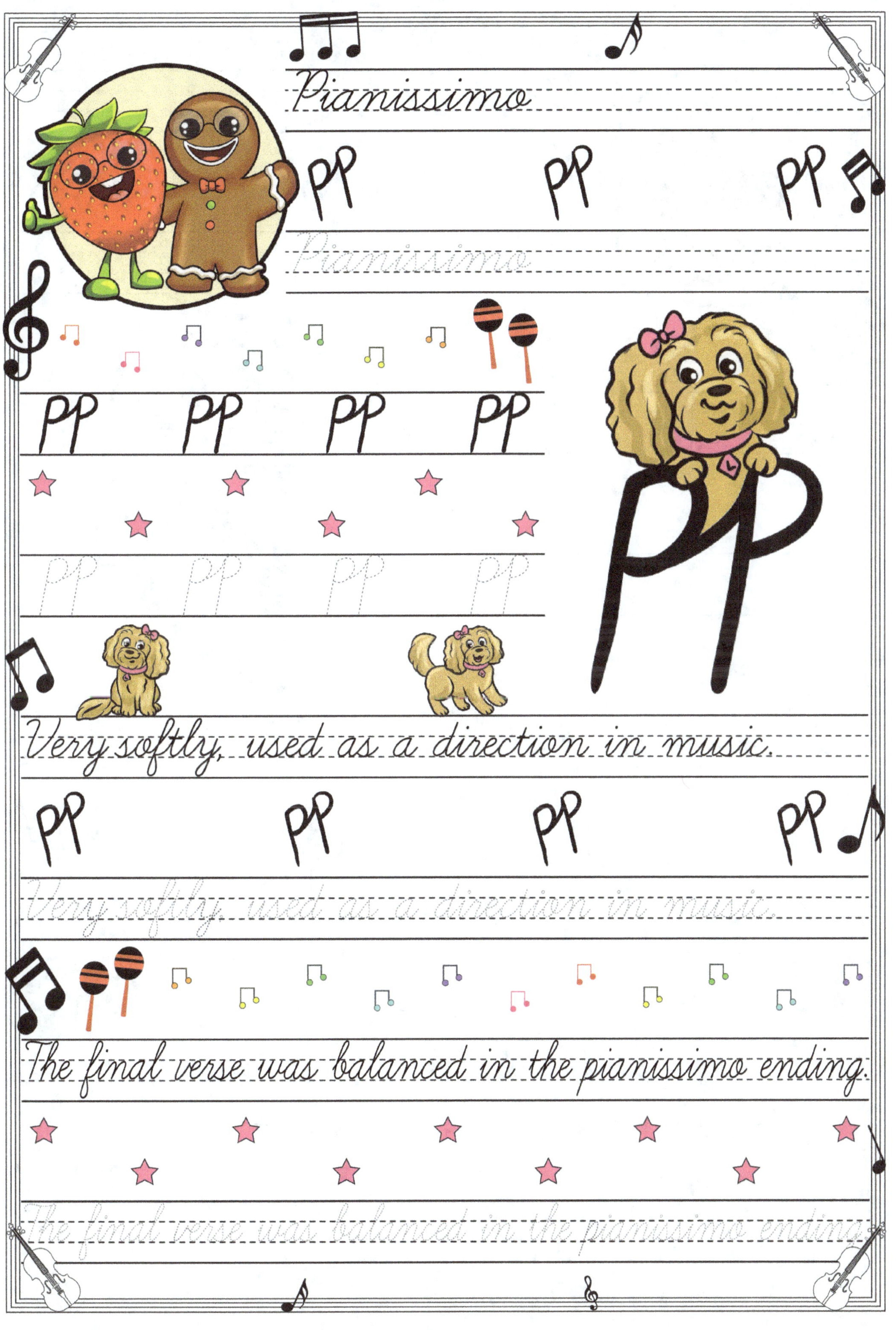

Pianissimo
PP   PP   PP
Pianissimo
PP   PP   PP   PP
PP
PP   PP   PP   PP
PP
Very softly, used as a direction in music.
PP   PP   PP   PP
Very softly, used as a direction in music.
The final verse was balanced in the pianissimo ending.
The final verse was balanced in the pianissimo ending.

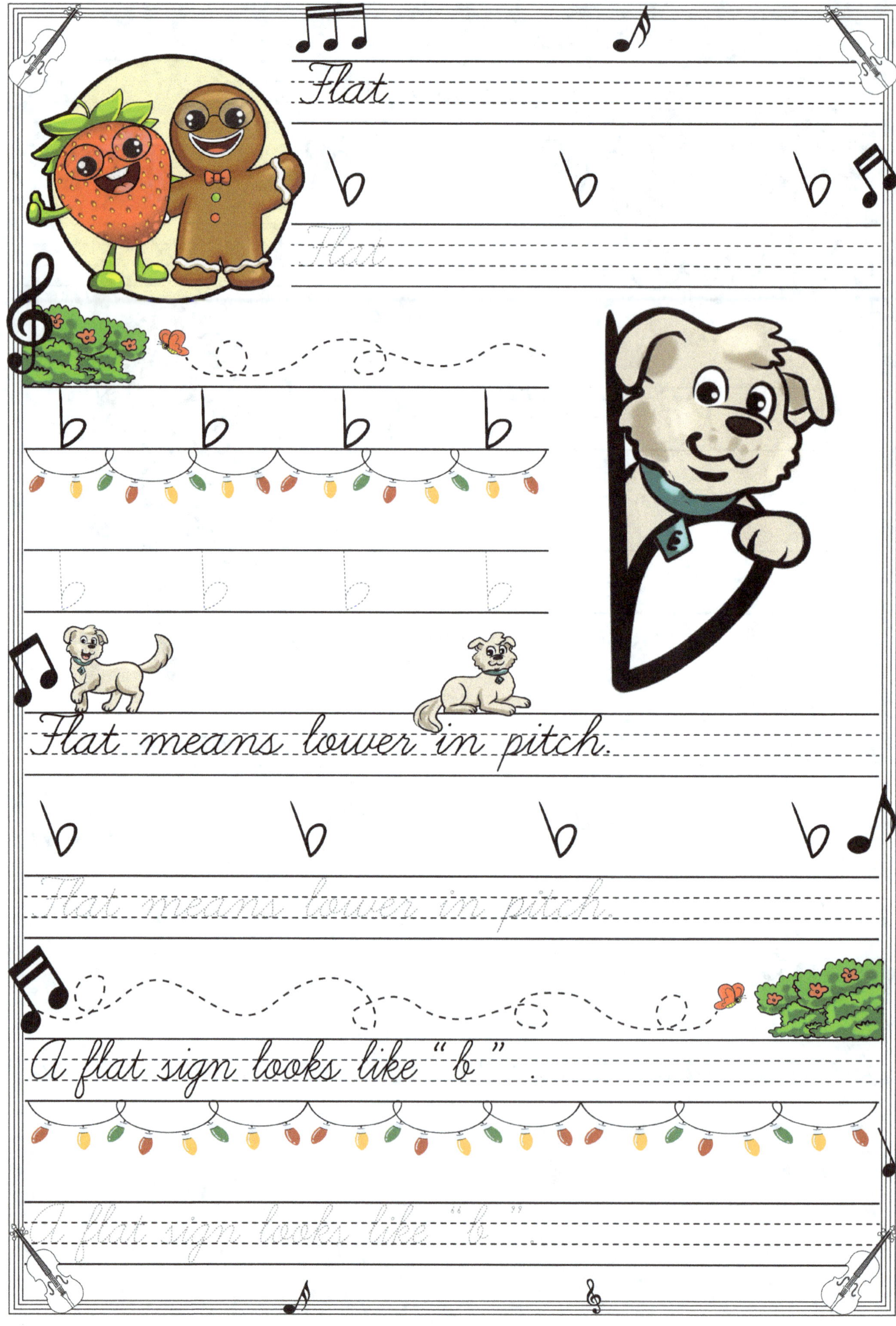

Flat
b   b   b
Flat
b   b   b   b
b   b   b   b
Flat means lower in pitch.
b   b   b   b
Flat means lower in pitch.
A flat sign looks like "b".
A flat sign looks like "b".

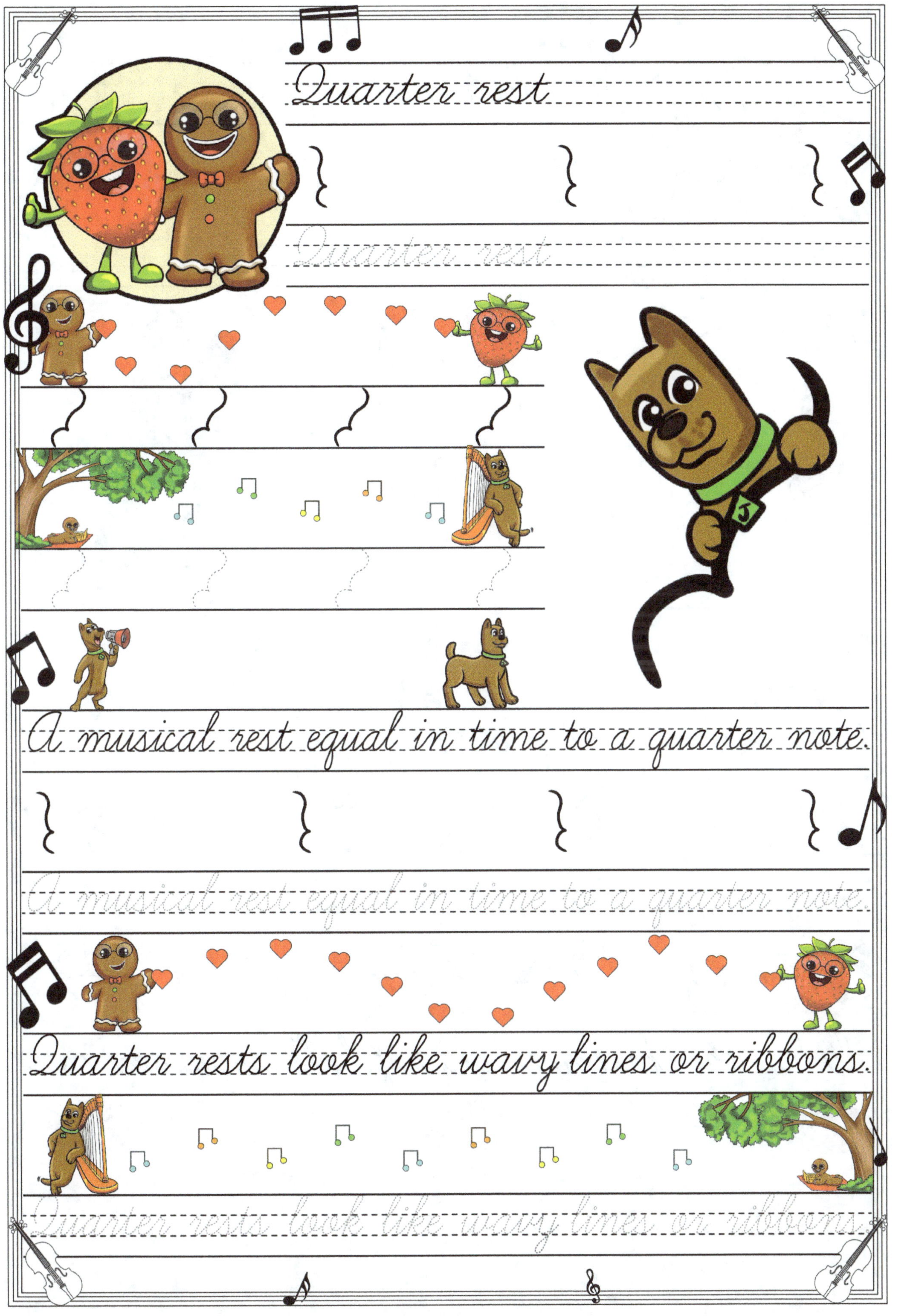

Quarter rest
A musical rest equal in time to a quarter note.
Quarter rests look like wavy lines or ribbons.

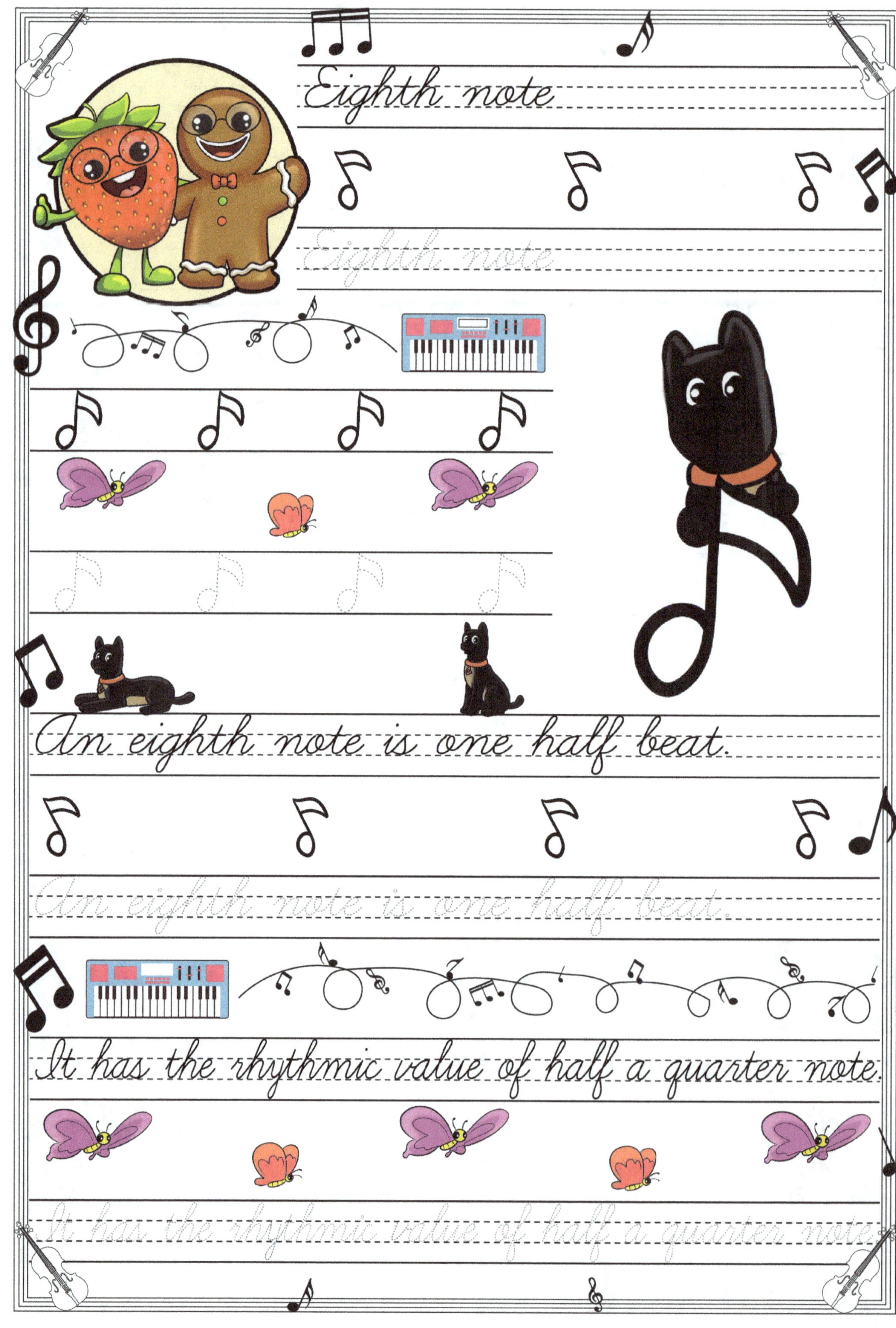
Eighth note
Eighth note
An eighth note is one half beat.
An eighth note is one half beat.
It has the rhythmic value of half a quarter note.
It has the rhythmic value of half a quarter note.

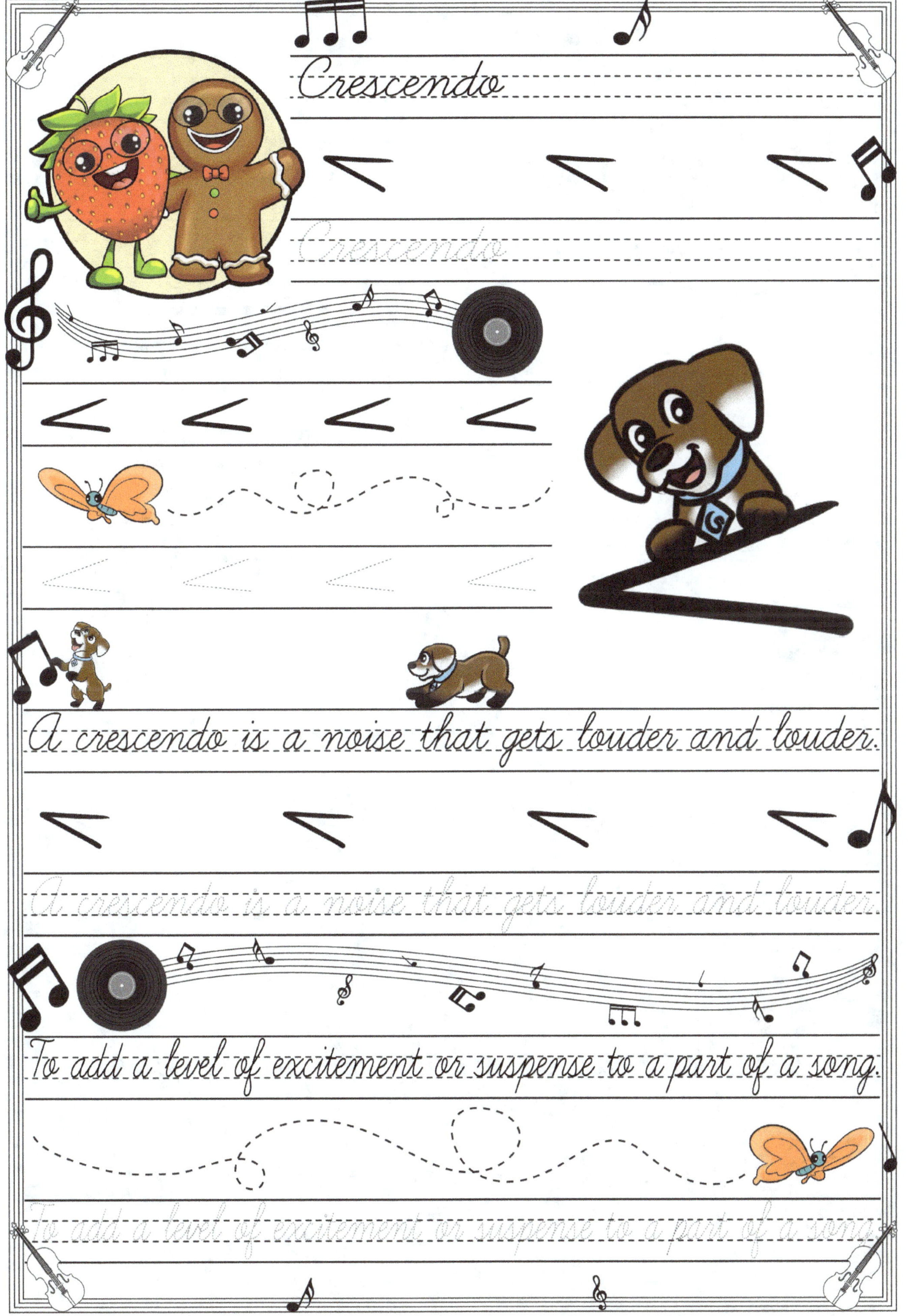

Crescendo
Crescendo
A crescendo is a noise that gets louder and louder.
A crescendo is a noise that gets louder and louder.
To add a level of excitement or suspense to a part of a song.
To add a level of excitement or suspense to a part of a song.

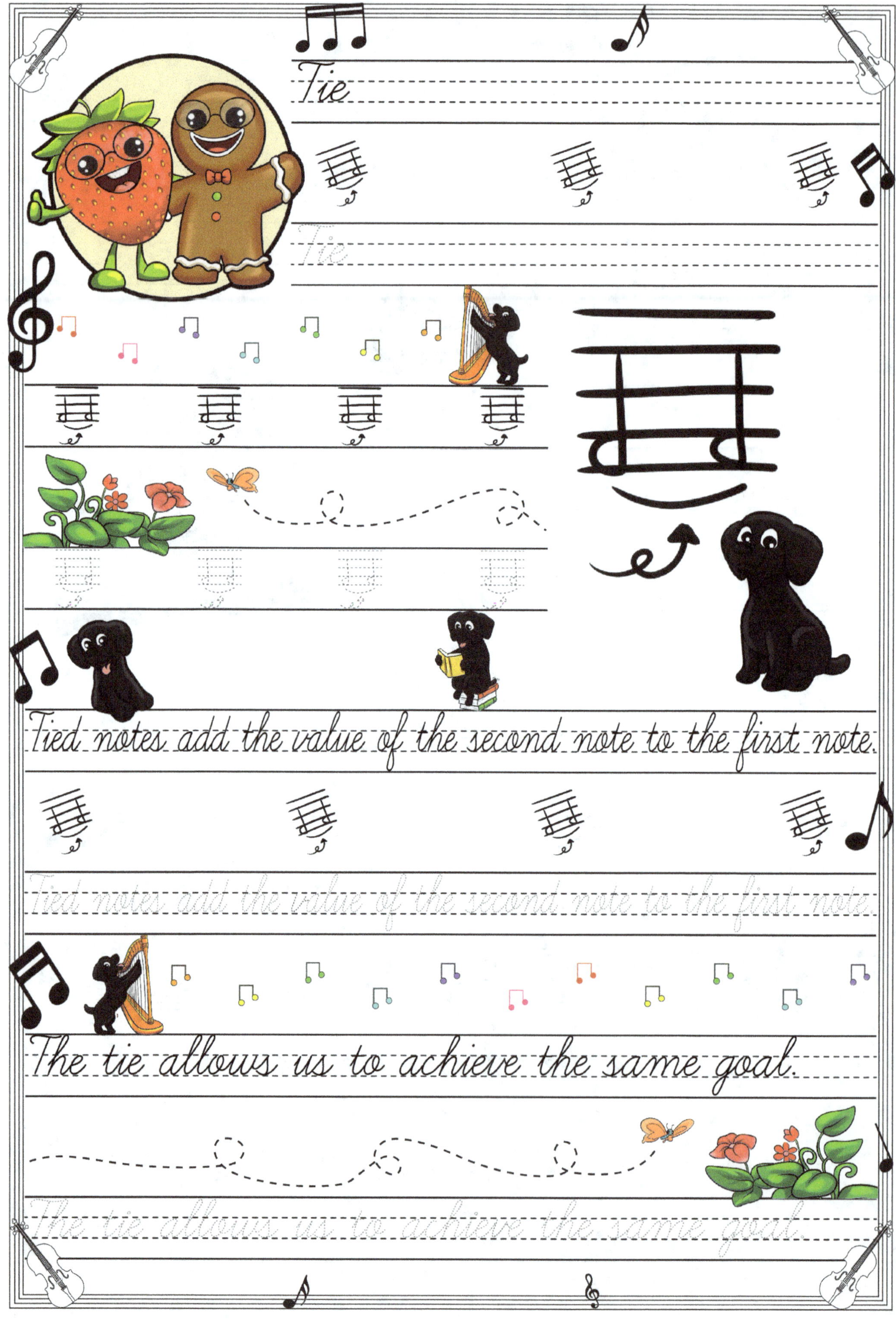

Tie

Tied notes add the value of the second note to the first note.

The tie allows us to achieve the same goal.

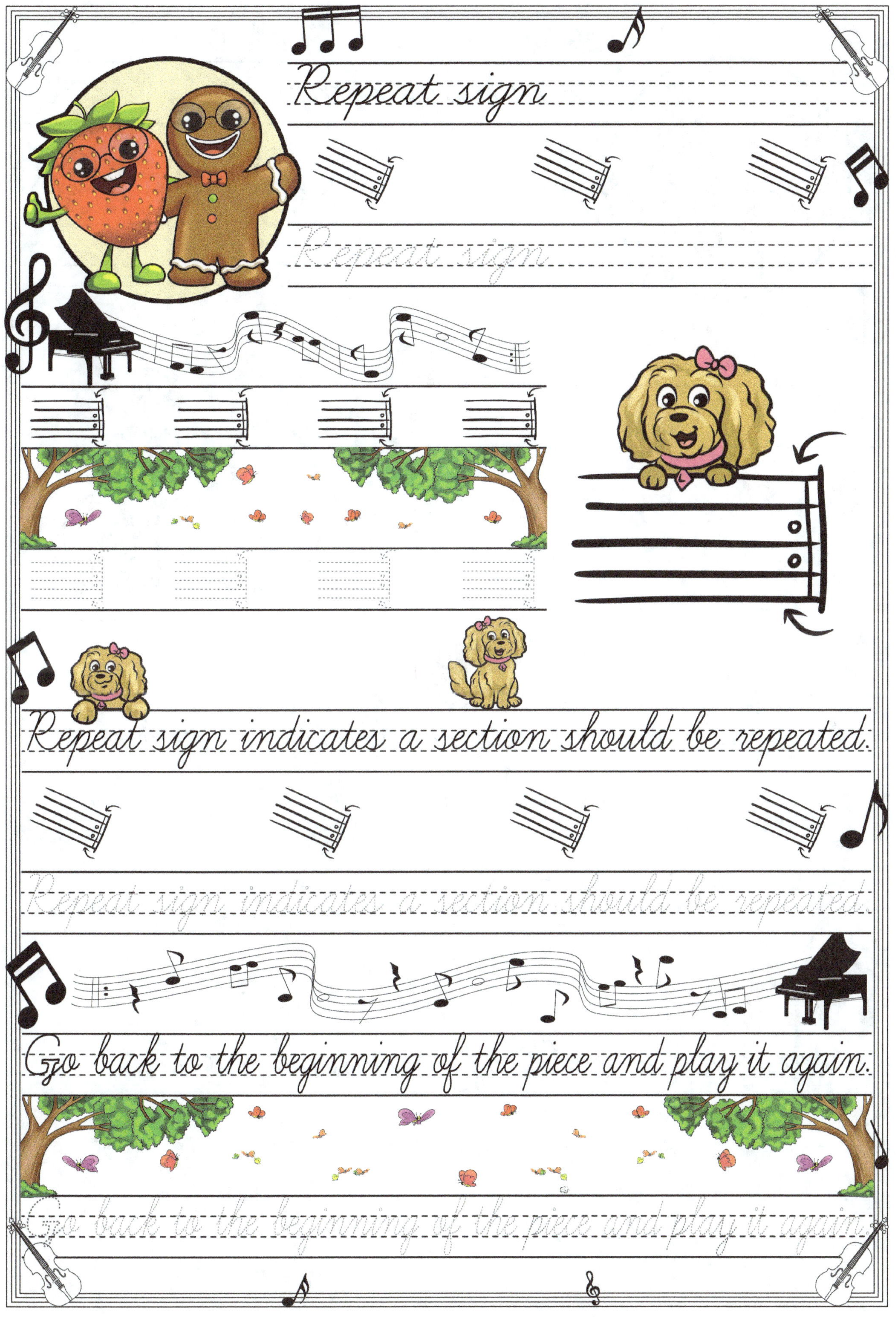

Repeat sign
Repeat sign
Repeat sign indicates a section should be repeated.
Repeat sign indicates a section should be repeated.
Go back to the beginning of the piece and play it again.
Go back to the beginning of the piece and play it again.

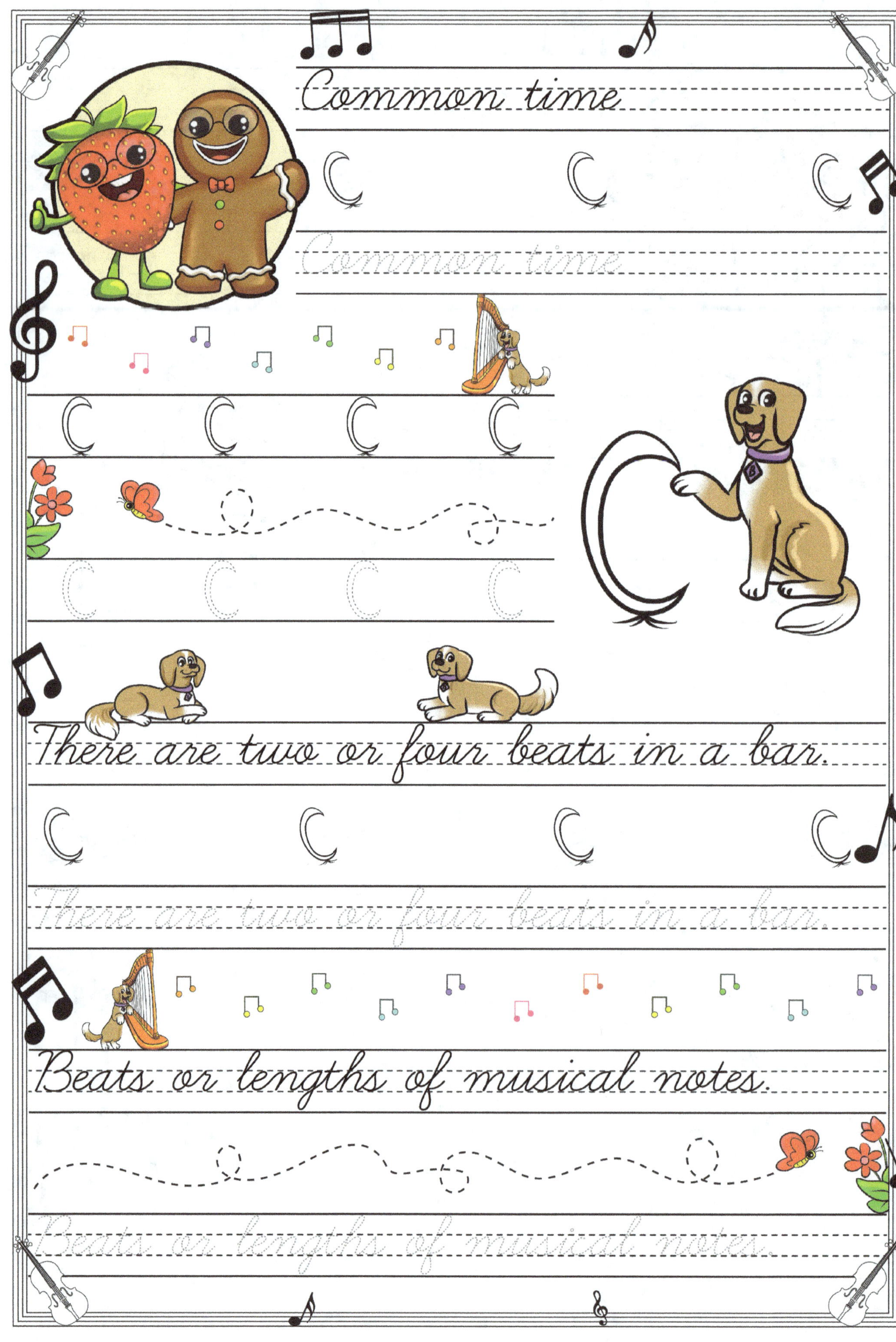

Common time

Common time

There are two or four beats in a bar.

There are two or four beats in a bar.

Beats or lengths of musical notes.

Beats or lengths of musical notes.

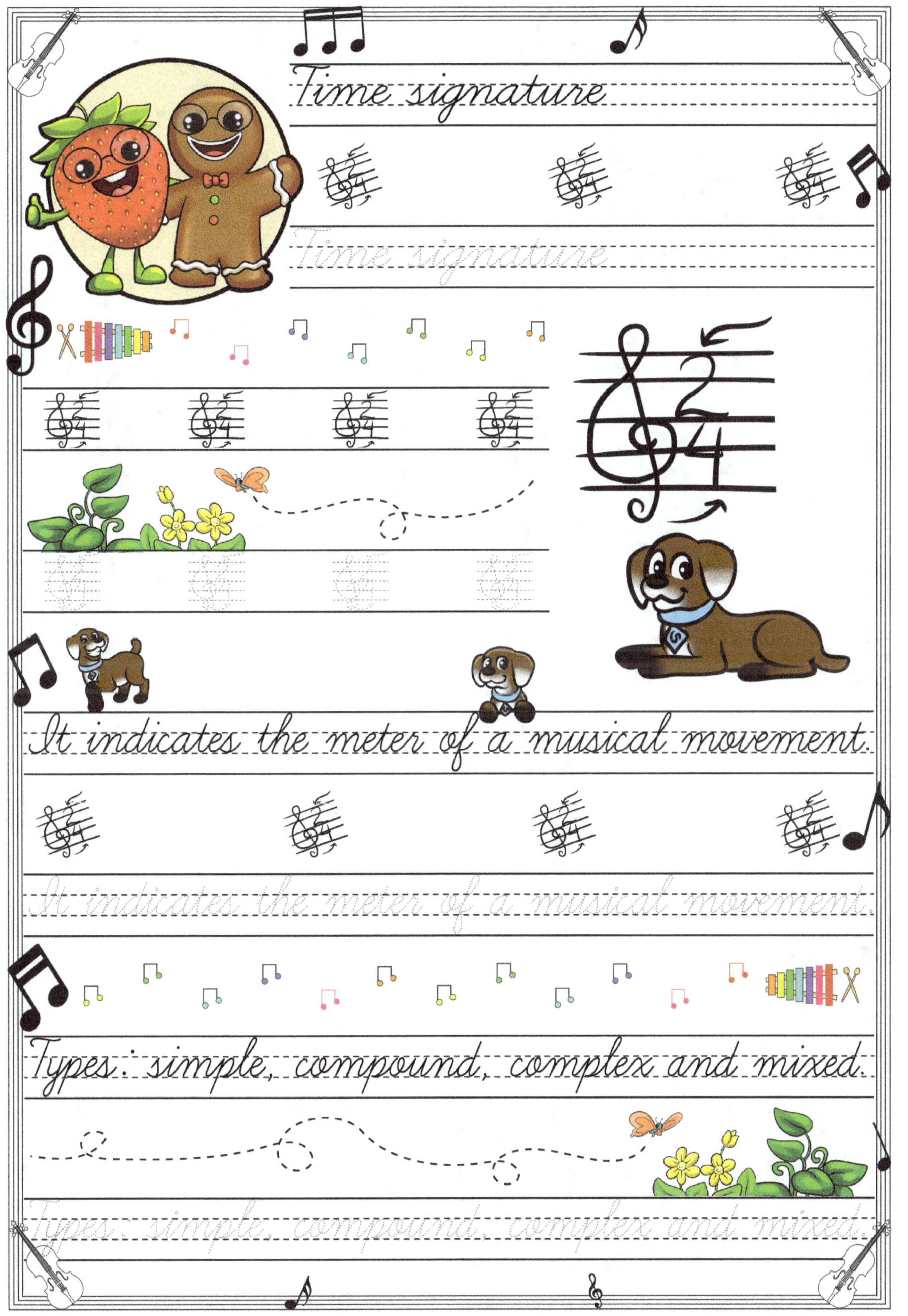

Time signature
Time signature
It indicates the meter of a musical movement.
It indicates the meter of a musical movement.
Types: simple, compound, complex and mixed.
Types: simple, compound, complex and mixed.

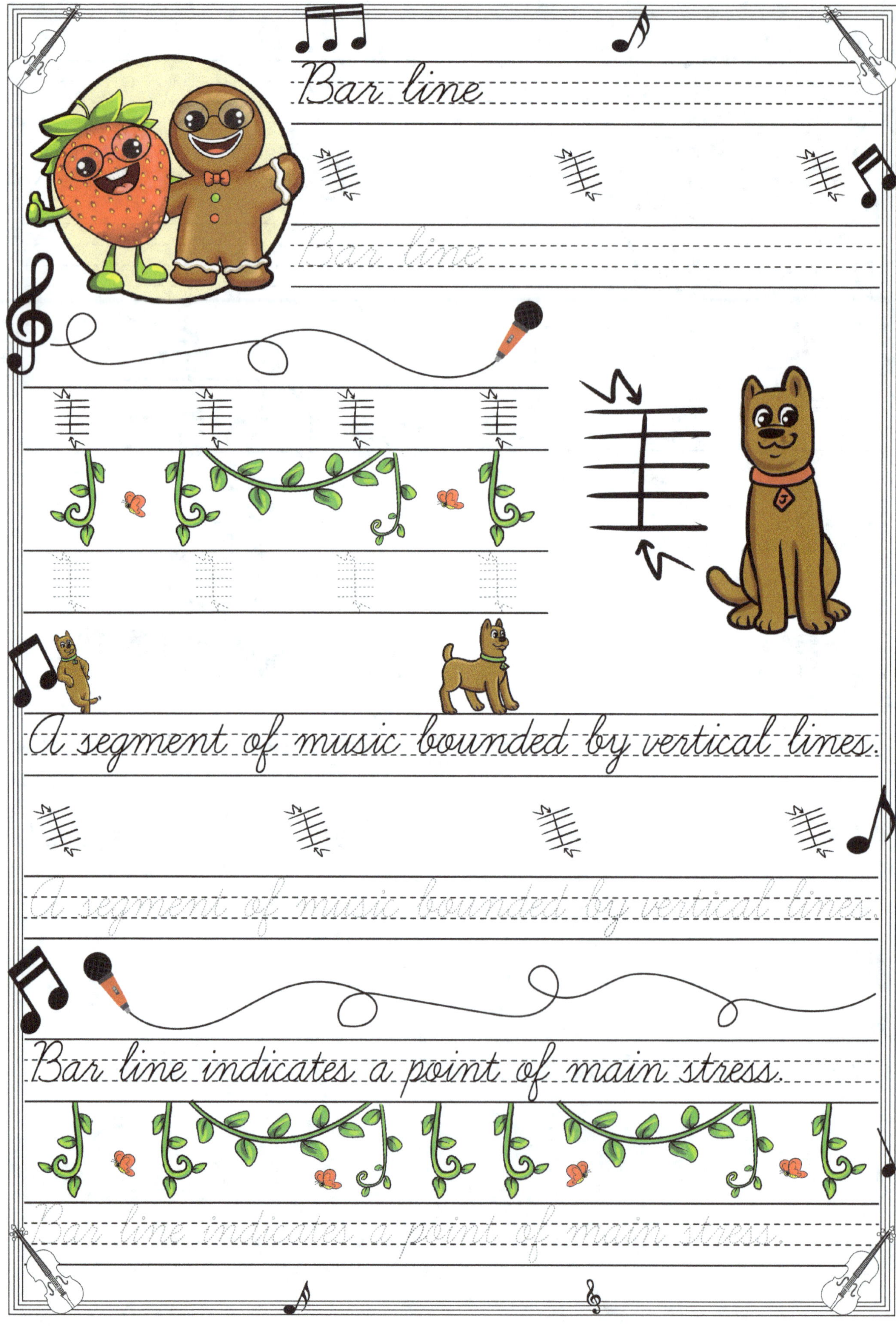
Bar line
Bar line
A segment of music bounded by vertical lines
A segment of music bounded by vertical lines
Bar line indicates a point of main stress.
Bar line indicates a point of main stress.

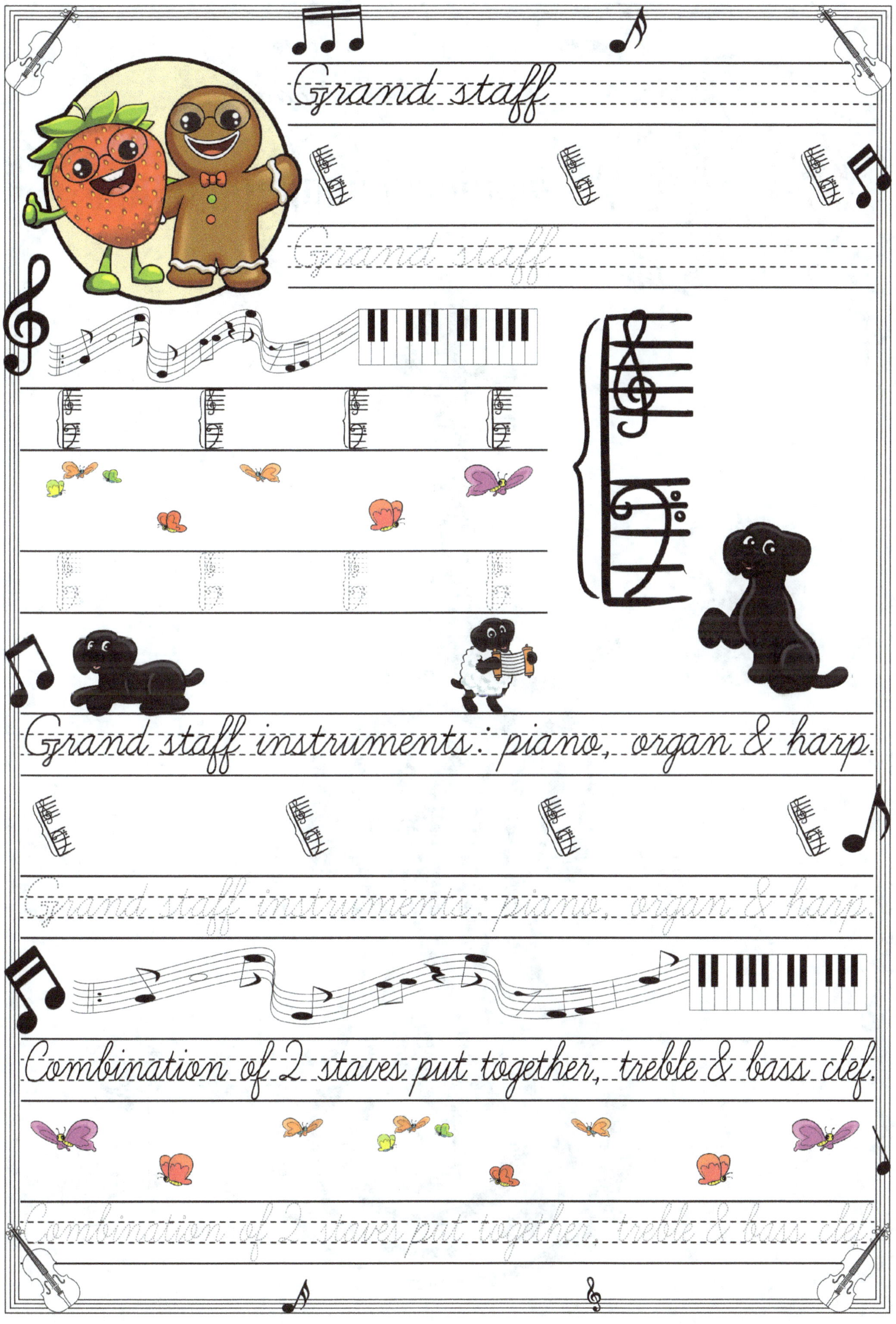

Grand staff
Grand staff
Grand staff instruments: piano, organ & harp.
Grand staff instruments: piano, organ & harp.
Combination of 2 staves put together, treble & bass clef.
Combination of 2 staves put together, treble & bass clef.

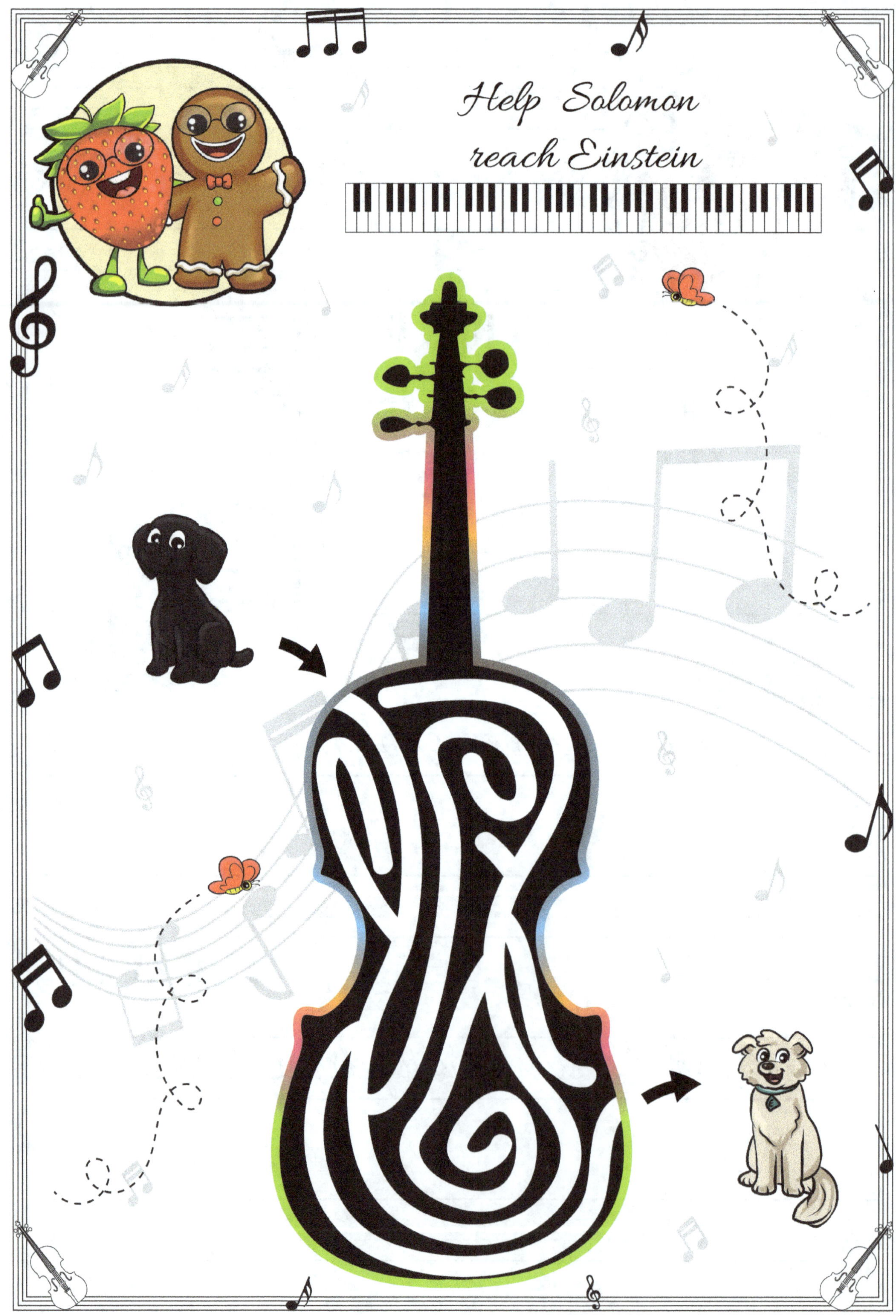

Help Solomon
reach Einstein

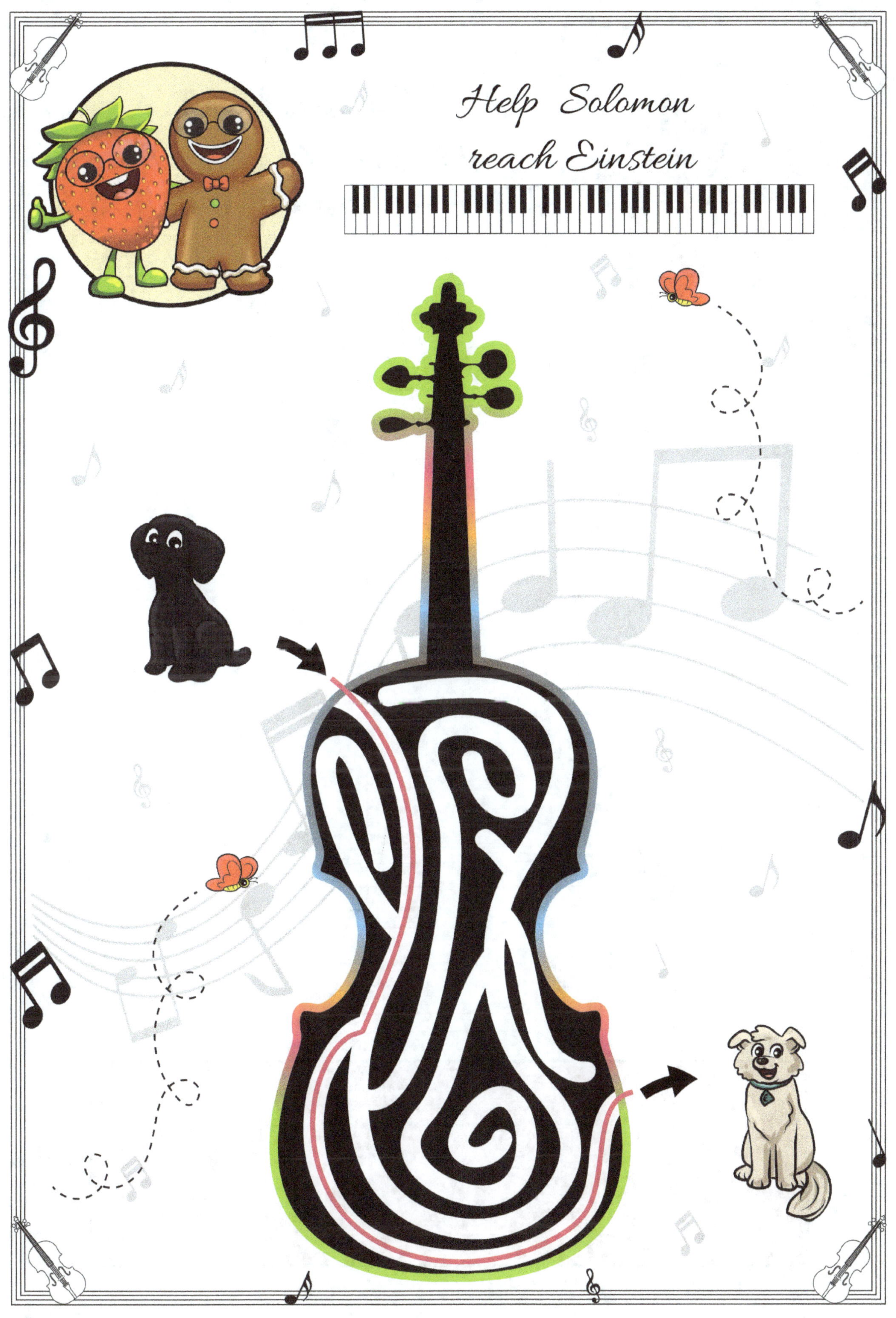
Help Solomon
reach Einstein

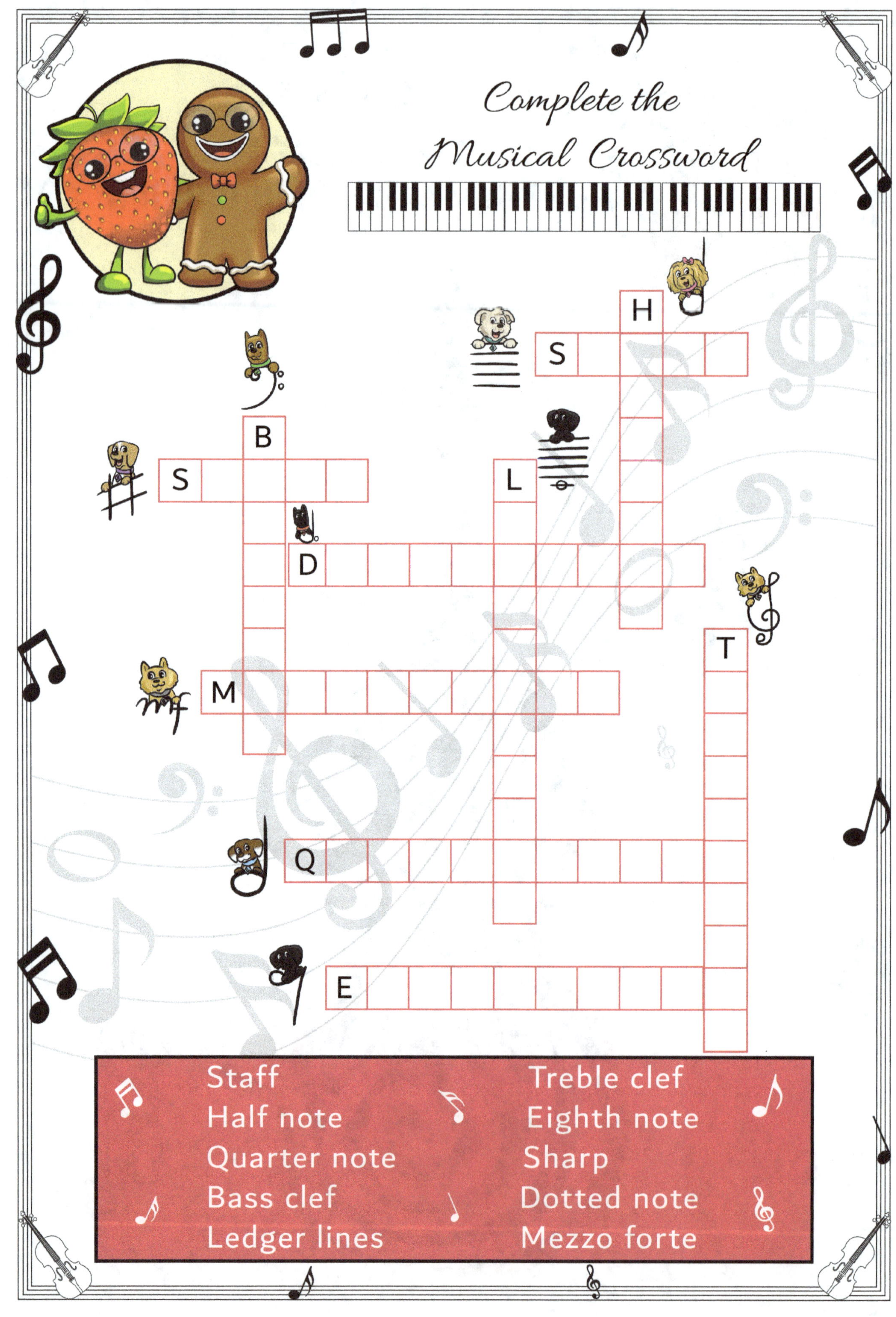

Complete the
Musical Crossword
H
S
B
S
L
D
M
T
Q
E
Staff
Half note
Quarter note
Bass clef
Ledger lines
Treble clef
Eighth note
Sharp
Dotted note
Mezzo forte

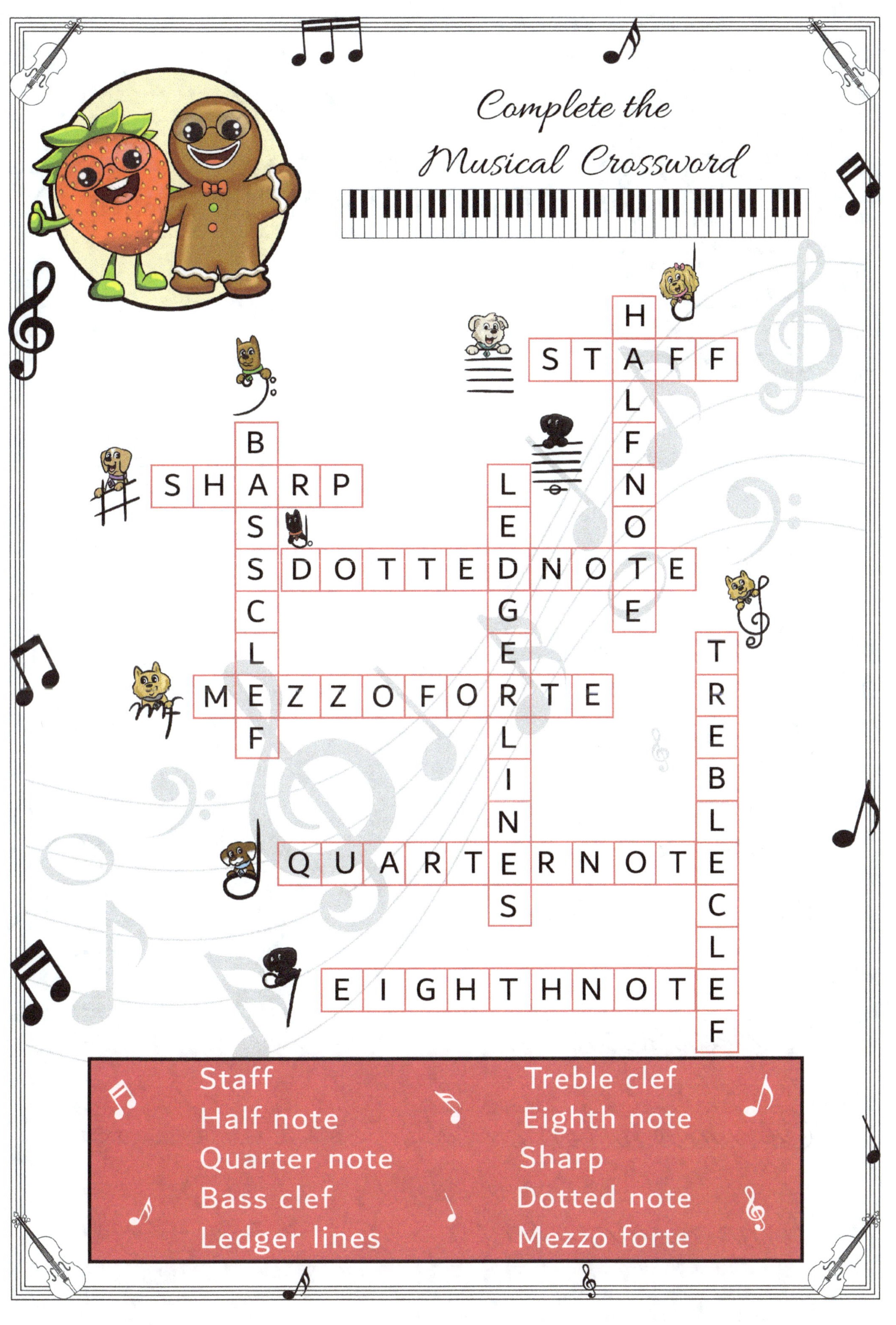
Complete the
Musical Crossword

H
S T A F F
A
L
B F
S H A R P N
A O
S D O T T E D N O T E T
C L E
L E D R
M E Z Z O F O R T E E
L B
G L
E E
R Q U A R T E R N O T E C
L L
I E
N F
E I G H T H N O T E F

Staff   Treble clef
Half note   Eighth note
Quarter note   Sharp
Bass clef   Dotted note
Ledger lines   Mezzo forte

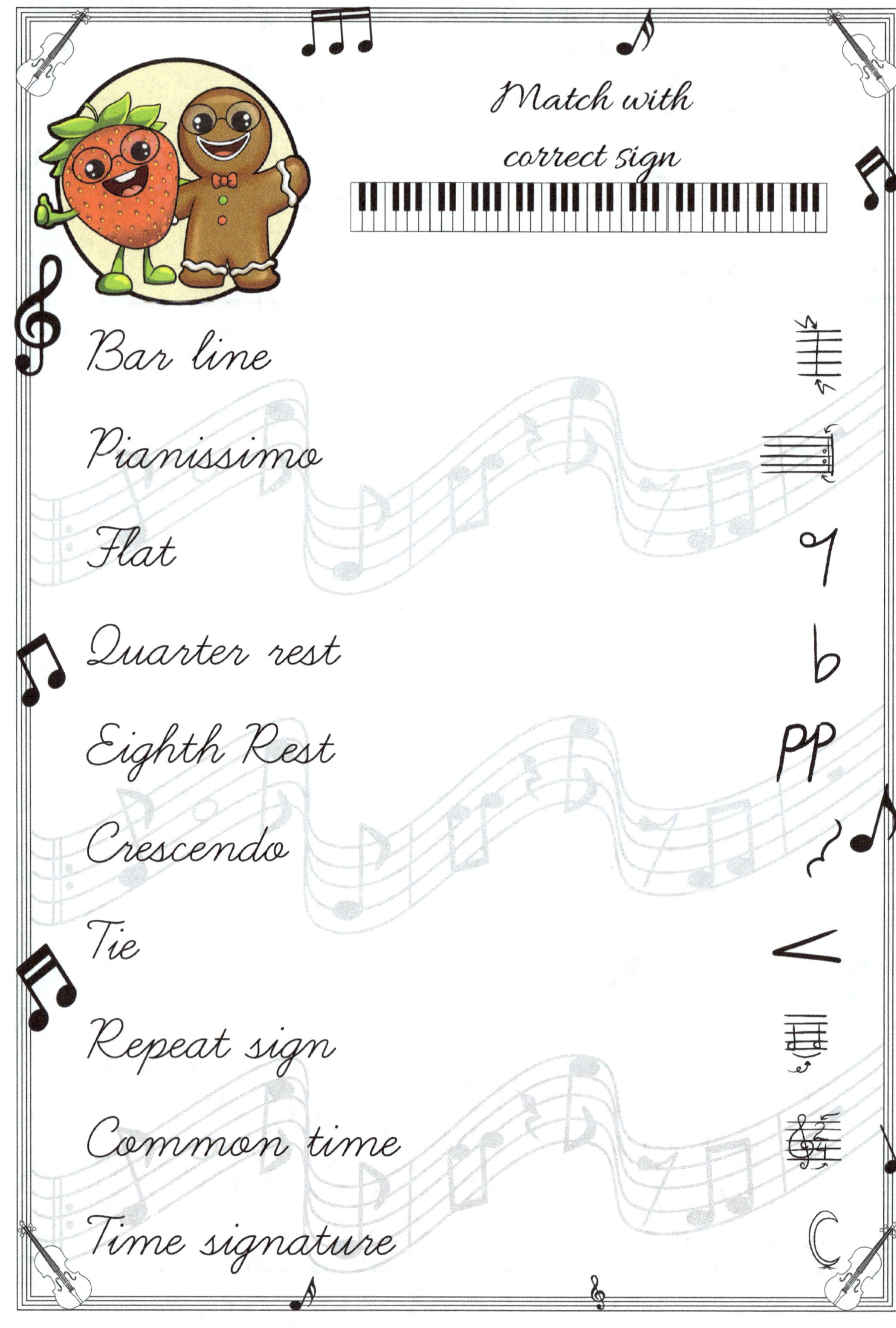

Match with
correct sign
Bar line
Pianissimo
Flat
Quarter rest
Eighth Rest
Crescendo
Tie
Repeat sign
Common time
Time signature
PP
C

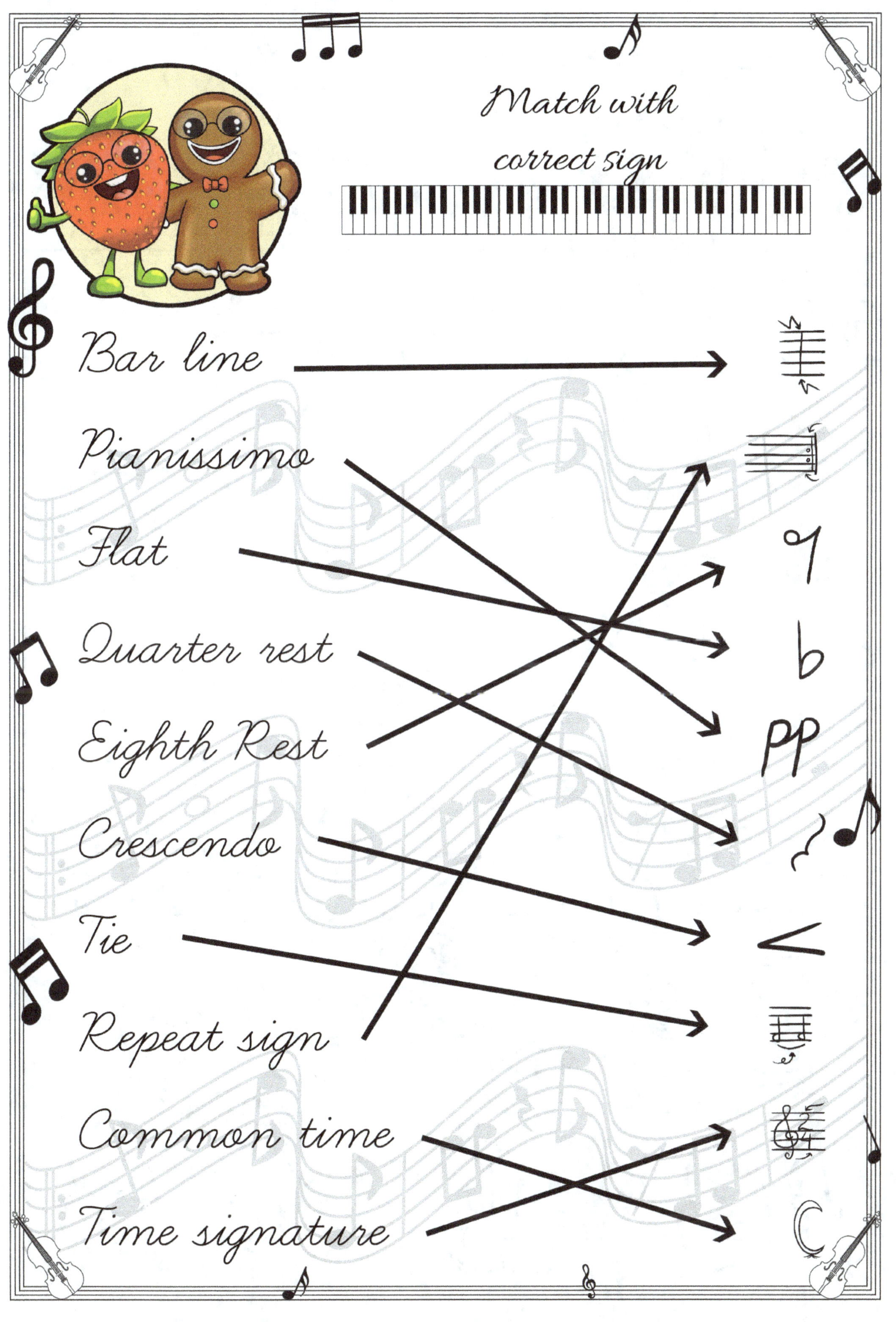

Match with
correct sign
Bar line
Pianissimo
Flat
Quarter rest
Eighth Rest
Crescendo
Tie
Repeat sign
Common time
Time signature
PP

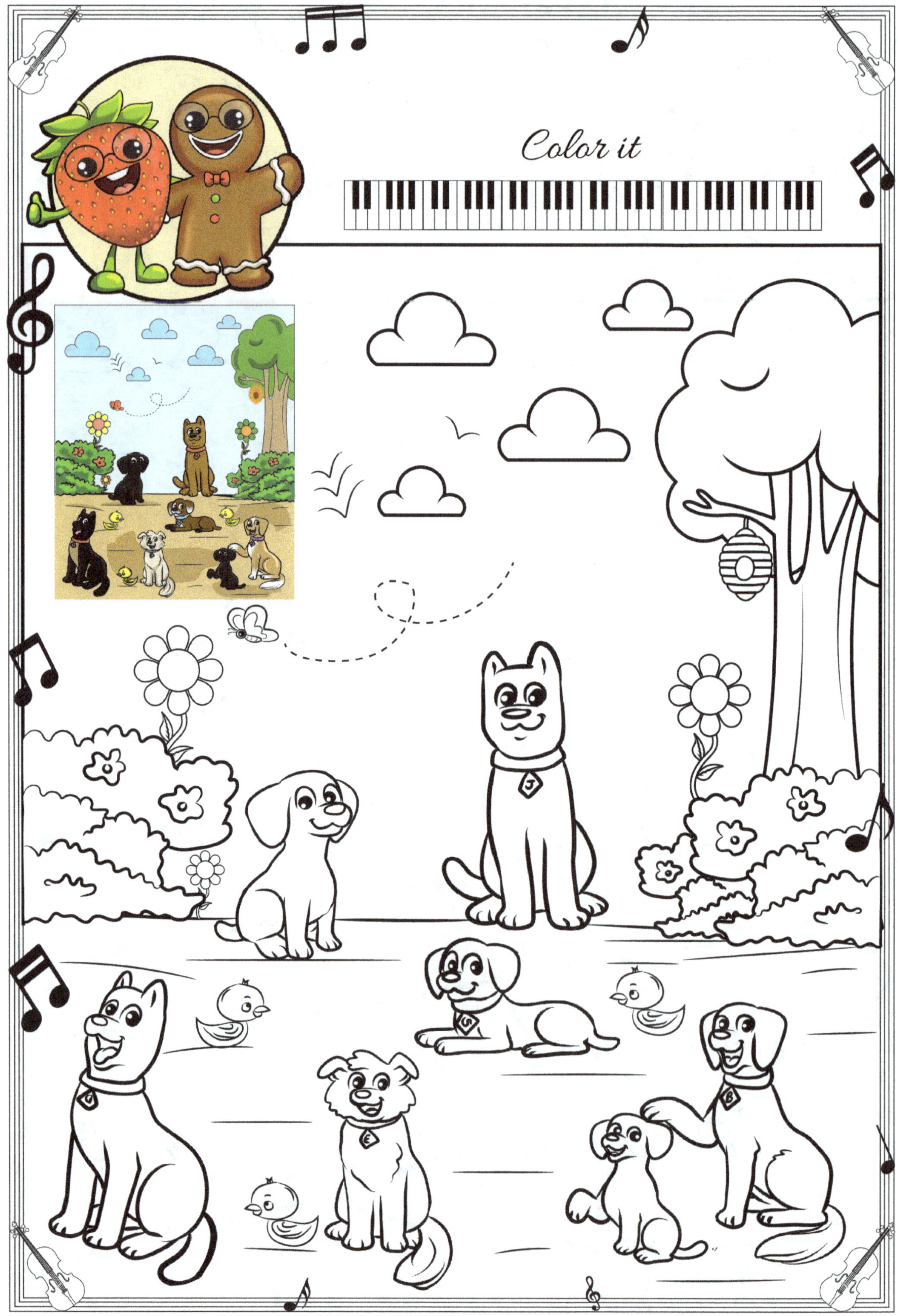
Color it

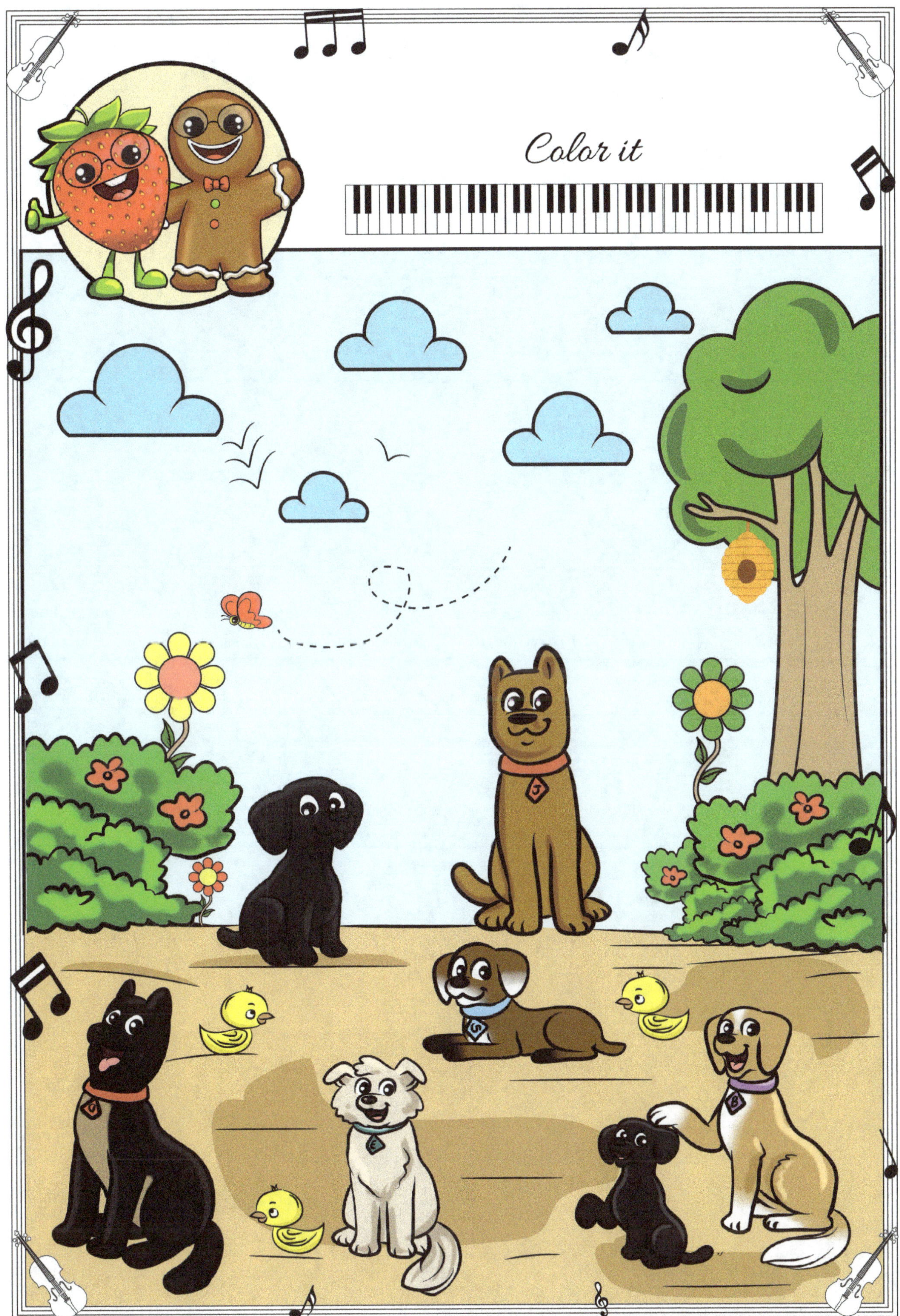
Color it